How to Be a Successful Student

How to Be a Successful Student is a clear, concise, evidence-based guide to the habits that are scientifically proven to help people learn. Acclaimed educational psychologist Richard Mayer distils cutting edge research to focus on the 20 best study habits for college students, including habits for motivating yourself to learn, managing your learning environment, and effectively applying learning strategies. This accessible, practical book covers all three areas with evidence-based, approachable suggestions to help you become a successful student by developing effective study habits and rejecting ineffective ones.

Richard E. Mayer is Distinguished Professor of Psychological and Brain Sciences at the University of California, Santa Barbara, USA. He served as President of Division 15 (Educational Psychology) of the American Psychological Association and Vice President of the American Educational Research Association for Division C (Learning and Instruction).

How to Be a Successful Student

20 Study Habits Based on the Science of Learning

Richard E. Mayer

Routledge
Taylor & Francis Group

NEW YORK AND LONDON

First published 2019
by Routledge
52 Vanderbilt Avenue, New York, NY 10017

and by Routledge
2 Park Square, Milton Park, Abingdon, Oxon, OX14 4RN

Routledge is an imprint of the Taylor & Francis Group, an informa business

Library of Congress Cataloging-in-Publication Data
A catalog record for this title has been requested

ISBN: 978-1-138-31985-1 (hbk)
ISBN: 978-1-138-31986-8 (pbk)
ISBN: 978-0-429-45374-8 (ebk)

Typeset in Stempel Garamond
by Apex CoVantage, LLC

Contents

Preface

The Book You Are Holding

The book you are holding is intended to help you become a successful college student. Perhaps you are reading it as part of a course on student success (or learning to learn) or as part of a summer bridge program offered by your college. In any case, by the time you finish reading this little book, my goal is that you will have the tools you need to improve how you learn in college courses and beyond. If you want to develop some research-based study habits that can make you a successful student, then this book is for you.

Learning to Learn as the Hidden Curriculum

In the United States, as in many countries around the world, we expect you to enter elementary school at about age five and leave high school 13 years later. If you are like the majority of high school graduates in the United States, your next step is to enter college. By the time you find yourself starting out in college, you have spent most of your life in school, honing your skills as a student. Throughout this long process, you are expected to know how to learn, but rarely does anyone actually take the time to teach you how to learn. This is why learning to learn is sometimes called the *hidden curriculum*: It is part of the curriculum because we expect you to learn it, and it is hidden because we do not actually teach it to you.

The transition from high school to college sometimes can help you recognize gaps in your knowledge of how to learn. Sub-optimal study techniques that were good enough for you to get by in elementary and high school may not be sufficient for success as you pursue higher education. That is where this book fits in.

Habits for Studying

The goal of this book is to help you improve your skills as a successful student, that is, to help you be more effective in academic learning. Becoming a successful student involves developing a coordinated collection of what I call *habits for studying*, including habits for how to motivate yourself to learn, how to manage your learning environment, and how to apply effective learning strategies. In this book, I summarize my 20 favorite evidence-based study habits—including four motivational habits, six management habits, and ten learning habits. I show how you can become a successful student by developing effective study habits and rejecting ineffective ones.

The demand for college courses in student success (or learning-to-learn courses) has been growing at community colleges and four-year colleges for decades, but the teaching of effective learning strategies still remains part of the hidden curriculum today. Perhaps you are taking just such a course right now. This book is my modest attempt to bring this valuable information out into the open, in order to help you in your continuing quest to become a successful learner.

How to Use This Book

This book is intended to help you become a better student, by equipping you with study habits that have been shown to improve learning in college students. You will learn about 20 study habits that have the potential to make you a better student, but you should focus on the ones that appeal most to you, mesh with your classes, and will give you the biggest boost. Try them out in your classes, and feel free to adjust them to suit your needs. In short, you can pick and choose the best habits for you, and you can tinker with them to make them your own. Overall, I recommend taking three steps to make the most of this book, based on each of the three parts of the book.

Step 1: Your first step is to develop a motive to improve your study skills. The first section of the book gives you four ways to develop the motivation you need for academic success—that is, four motivational habits. First, take some time to explain why you are interested in becoming a better student—How does this book have any value for me? Second, articulate your goals as a college student—Do you want to do a better job of understanding the material, and do you want to get good grades?

Third, decide whether you think you can improve your study skills by putting some effort into engaging with this book—Do you see yourself as capable of learning the material in your classes? Finally, confront negative stereotypes: Are you letting other people's negative beliefs affect the way you see yourself as a learner? In short, a major goal of the first section of the book is to help you develop productive beliefs about yourself. Try to come away from Part 1 with a firm motive to improve as a student: Being able to see value in what you are learning and being able to see yourself as a competent learner who can master the material if you work hard enough.

Step 2: Your second step is to develop an opportunity to improve your learning. Part 2 shows you how to manage your time, how to create a distraction-free zone for studying, and how to clear your head of worry and mind wandering. You don't need to implement every suggestion in Part 2, but you should try to come away from Part 2 with a set of management habits that fit your personal style—including habits for scheduling your study time, for finding a calm place to study, and for focusing your attention on the task of learning.

Step 3: Your third step is to develop some learning habits (or strategies) that fit your personal style and the demands of the courses you are taking. Part 3 offers ten learning habits ranging from outlining the material in a chapter or lecture to trying to teach yourself the material in a chapter or lecture. I suggest that you try to come away from Part 3 with at least three primary learning habits that you are committed to using, and maybe a couple more that you plan to try. You don't need to use all of them all of the time, but you should settle on a few learning habits that add to your success as a student.

In short, I hope this book will help you add a few useful study habits to your collection—ones that you feel comfortable using and that have a positive impact on your learning. If this book helps you improve your success as a student, even just a little bit, then I will consider it to be a success.

The Power of Learning Strategies

I have been writing this book in my head during the past 30 years (and it has been giving me quite a headache). Back in the 1980s, research on learning strategies had progressed to the point that we thought learning strategy instruction would become a fundamental part of K-12 education, but so far that has not happened. My first comprehensive look at the power of learning strategies was a 1986 chapter on "The teaching of learning strategies" in the *Handbook of Research on Teaching* by Claire Weinstein and me, where we made the case for teaching of learning strategies and summarized research evidence on eight types of learning strategies. My first research study on learning strategies (with Linda Cook in 1988) involved teaching community college students how to outline their science textbooks based on organizing structures such as generalization (i.e., assertion and supporting evidence), enumeration (i.e., concept with a list of characteristics), and sequence (i.e., steps in a process). I was impressed with the power of learning strategies when we discovered that the training resulted in substantial improvements on learning outcome tests as compared to a control group. This gave me some confidence that there just might be something useful about teaching learning strategies to college students.

Subsequently, my colleagues (including Richard Peper and Kenneth Kiewra) and I continued to conduct a series of research studies demonstrating the power of notetaking to improve academic learning in college students, again reinforcing my confidence. More recently, a series of research studies by Hector Ponce, his collaborators, and myself has shown the value of teaching learning strategies such as mapping (i.e., creating a spatial arrangement of the key ideas) and highlighting (i.e., marking the main points in a text) in improving test performance. By using eye-tracking methodology we could show how these kinds of learning strategies cause students to process the material more deeply. By conducting studies in school settings we could see that teaching of learning strategies works to improve academic performance in the real world of students. By embedding these strategies in a computer interface we could show that study strategies also apply to computer-based learning.

I also have been impressed with our recent research findings showing that students learn better when they draw diagrams to depict the material in a text (with Annett

Schmeck and colleagues), when they imagine diagrams to depict the material in a text (with Claudia Leopold and colleagues), when they explain the material to others by making a video lecture (with Logan Fiorella), when they are asked to explain the material to themselves during learning (with Cheryl Johnson), when they test themselves on the material they just studied (with Cheryl Johnson), or when they write a summary of what they are learning (with Logan Fiorella, with Jocelyn Parong, and with Celeste Pilegard).

My interest in learning strategies culminated in our 2015 book (by Logan Fiorella and myself) entitled *Learning as a generative activity: Eight learning strategies that promote understanding,* which summarized eight learning strategies that have a solid evidence base. Thus, as you can see, taking an evidence-based approach to the teaching of learning strategies has been on my research agenda for the past 30 years. In the book you are holding, I wanted to translate that solid research base into a practical guide for how to study aimed mainly at beginning college students.

From my vantage point as an educational psychologist who has been studying how to help people learn for decades in the Department of Psychological and Brain Sciences at the University of California, Santa Barbara, this is an exciting time. In my humble opinion, we are making important progress in applying the science of learning to education, which has been the continuing goal of educational psychologists for more than a century. Today, educational psychology equips us with research-based theories of how learning and motivation work in academic settings, and with converging scientific evidence concerning successful learning strategies. Instead of basing my advice on opinions or fads or ideology, I strive to take an evidence-based approach in this book. However, I must acknowledge that some of my advice in the "So What Should I Do?" section of each chapter needs further research investigation.

In short, my years of experience with research on learning strategies has turned me into a strong advocate for teaching students how to study. In this book, I share with you my evidence-based advice in hopes that it will help you become a better learner. Thus, a distinguishing feature of this book is that it is based on evidence rather than opinion and is written by someone who has been conducting and publishing research on learning strategies for the past three decades.

I have to admit that writing this book turned out to be a lot more fun than I expected it to be. I decided to form each chapter around a scenario comparing successful and unsuccessful study habits. My rationale for comparing successful and unsuccessful strategies is that sometimes you need to see the wrong way to do things in order to improve your skill at doing them the right way. In short, I want you to increase your skill at becoming a successful academic learner. Please feel free to communicate with me at mayer@psych.ucsb.edu if you have any thoughts on how I could improve this book or on new study habits I could add.

Acknowledgements

I wish to acknowledge grant support from the Office of Naval Research (including Award N000141612046), which has helped fund some of the research that instigated my interest in writing this book.

I also wish to thank the helpful editorial staff at Routledge including Alex Masulis, Heather Jarrow, and Lauren Frankfurt.

Although I am listed as the author, the ideas in this book were shaped by many researchers and scholars in the field of learning strategies, including students and colleagues that I have had the privilege of working with and learning from over the years. In particular, in addition to my graduate mentor, Jim Greeno, I wish to thank Bob Bjork, Elizabeth Bjork, Linda Cook, John Dunlosky, Logan Fiorella, Silvie Huang, Cheryl Johnson, Ken Kiewra, Claudia Leopold, Joel Levin, Mark McDaniel, Kathleen McDermott, Jocelyn Parong, Hal Pashler, Rick Peper, Celeste Pilegard, Hector Ponce, Mike Pressley, Roddy Roediger, Annett Schmeck, Tom Stahovich, Merl Wittrock, and Claire Weinstein. I appreciate the support of my parents, James and Bernis Mayer, who are always in my thoughts, as well as my brothers, Bob and Bernie Mayer. My children (Ken, Dave, and Sarah) and grandchildren (Jacob, Avery, James, Emma, Caleb, Sophie, and Lily) fill my life with joy and pride. I owe a special thanks to my wife, Beverly, who is my constant source of support.

Who Am I?

Let me introduce myself. I entered preschool when I was 3 years old and have been in school ever since. I attended Cincinnati public schools from kindergarten through twelfth grade, then received a B.A. degree in psychology from Miami University (in Oxford, Ohio) and a M.S. and Ph.D. in psychology from the University of Michigan (in Ann Arbor). After a two-year stint as a Visiting Assistant Professor of Psychology at Indiana University, I landed my dream job at the University of California, Santa Barbara, where now I am a Distinguished Professor of Psychological and Brain Sciences.

My research interests are in applying the science of learning to education, with a focus on how to help people learn in ways so they can transfer what they have learned to new situations. My research is at the intersection of cognition, instruction, and technology, with current projects on learning strategies, multimedia learning, computer-supported learning, and computer games for learning.

Over the years, my colleagues have been kind enough to honor my research contributions with various lifetime achievement awards: the E. L. Thorndike Award for career achievement in educational psychology (from Division 15 of the American Psychological Association), the Silvia Scribner Award for outstanding research in learning and instruction (from Division C of the American Educational Research Association), the David Jonassen Award for excellence in research in the field of instructional design and technology (from the Association for Educational Communications and Technology), the James McKeen Cattell Award for a lifetime of outstanding contributions to applied psychological research (from the Association for Psychological Science), and the Distinguished Contribution of Applications of Psychology to Education and Training Award (from the American Psychological Association). I was ranked #1 as the most productive educational psychologist in the world in *Contemporary Educational Psychology* and #1 as the most cited educational psychologist in Google Scholar.

Along the way, I served as President of Division 15 (Educational Psychology) of the American Psychological Association and Vice President of the American Educational Research Association for Division C (Learning and Instruction). During my research career, I have served as Principal Investigator or co-PI on more than 35 grants, including current grants from the Spencer Foundation, the Office of Naval Research, the Institute of Education Sciences, and the National Science Foundation. I am the former editor of the *Educational Psychologist* and former co-editor of *Instructional Science,* and I currently serve on the editorial boards of 12 journals, mainly in educational psychology.

I am the author of more than 500 publications including 30 books mainly aimed at applying the science of learning to education, such as *Learning as a Generative Activity*, *Computer Games for Learning*, *Applying the Science of Learning*, *e-Learning and the Science of Instruction: Fourth Edition* (with R. Clark), *Multimedia Learning: Second Edition*, *Learning and Instruction: Second Edition*, *Handbook of Research on Learning and Instruction: Second Edition* (co-editor with P. Alexander), and *The Cambridge Handbook of Multimedia Learning: Second Edition* (editor).

I love to learn and want you to improve your skills as a successful learner—based on research evidence from the science of learning.

Richard E. Mayer
Santa Barbara, CA

Selected Bibliography of Our Work on Learning Strategies

Weinstein, C. E., & Mayer, R. E. (1986). The teaching of learning strategies. In M. C. Wittrock (Ed.), *Handbook of Research on Teaching, Third Edition* (pp. 315–327), New York: Macmillan.

Peper, R. J., & Mayer, R. E. (1986). Generative effects of note taking during science lectures. *Journal of Educational Psychology, 78*, 23–28.

Cook, L. K., & Mayer, R E. (1988). Teaching readers about the structure of scientific text. *Journal of Educational Psychology, 80*, 448–456.

Shrager, L., & Mayer, R. E. (1989). Notetaking fosters generative learning strategies in novices. *Journal of Educational Psychology, 81*, 263–264.

Kiewra, K., Mayer, R. E., Christian, D., Dyreson, M., & McShane, A. (1991). Effects of repetition on recall and notetaking: Strategies for learning from lectures. *Journal of Educational Psychology, 82*, 120–123.

Johnson, C. I., & Mayer, R. E. (2009). A testing effect with multimedia learning. *Journal of Educational Psychology, 101*, 621–629.

Johnson, C. I., & Mayer, R. E. (2010). Adding the self-explanation principle to multimedia learning in a computer-based game-like environment. *Computers in Human Behavior, 26*, 1246–1252.

Mayer, R. E., & Johnson, C. I. (2010). Adding instructional features that promote learning in a game-like environment. *Journal of Educational Computing Research, 42*, 241–265.

Schwamborn, A., Mayer, R. E., Thillmann, H., Leopold, C., & Leutner, D. (2010). Drawing as a generative activity and drawing as a prognostic activity. *Journal of Educational Psychology, 102*, 872–879.

Fiorella, L., & Mayer, R. E. (2012). Paper-based aids for learning with a computer-based game. *Journal of Educational Psychology, 104*, 1074–1082.

Ponce, H. R., Lopez, M. J., & Mayer, R. E. (2012). Instructional effectiveness of a computer-supported program for teaching reading comprehension strategies. *Computers & Education, 59*, 1170–1183.

Fiorella, L., & Mayer, R. E. (2013). The relative benefits of learning by teaching and teaching expectancy. *Contemporary Educational Psychology, 38*, 281–288.

Fiorella, L., & Mayer, R. E. (2014). The role of explanations and expectations in learning by teaching. *Contemporary Educational Psychology, 39*, 75–85.

Ponce, H. R., & Mayer, R. E. (2014). Qualitatively different cognitive processing during online reading primed by different study activities. *Computers in Human Behavior, 30*, 121–130.

Ponce, H., & Mayer, R. E. (2014). An eye–movement analysis of highlighting and graphic organizer study aids for learning from expository text. *Computers in Human Behavior, 41* 21–32.

Schmeck, A., Mayer, R. E., Opfermann, M., Pfeiffer, V., & Leutner, D. (2014). Drawing pictures during learning from scientific text: Testing the generative drawing effect and the prognostic drawing effect. *Contemporary Educational Psychology, 39*, 275–286.

Fiorella, L., & Mayer, R. E. (2015). *Learning as a generative activity: Eight learning strategies that promote understanding.* New York: Cambridge University Press.

Leopold, C., & Mayer, R. E. (2015). An imagination effect in learning from scientific text. *Journal of Educational Psychology, 107,* 47–63.

Fiorella, L. & Mayer, R. E. (2016). Eight ways to promote generative learning. *Educational Psychology Review, 28,* 717–741.

Pilegard, C., & Mayer, R. E. (2016). Improving academic learning from computer-based narrative games. *Contemporary Educational Psychology, 44,* 12–20.

Fiorella, L., & Mayer, R. E. (2017). Spontaneous spatial strategies in learning from scientific text. *Contemporary Educational Psychology, 49,* 66–79.

Rawson, K., Stahovich, T. F., & Mayer, R. E. (2017). Homework and achievement: Using smartpen technology to find the connection. *Journal of Educational Psychology, 109,* 208–219.

Gyllen, J., Stahovich, T., & Mayer, R. E. (in press). How students read an e-textbook in an engineering course. *Journal of Computer Assisted Learning.*

Huang, X., & Mayer, R. E. (in press). Adding self-efficacy features to an online statistics lesson. *Journal of Educational Computing Research.*

Parong, J., & Mayer, R. E. (in press). Learning science in immersive virtual reality. *Journal of Educational Psychology.*

Introduction

Academic Success Depends on MOM: Motive, Opportunity, and Means

Who Done It?

It's 10:50 pm and you are sitting blissfully in front of your TV, watching the final minutes of a gripping crime drama. The defendant—an unlikable character named Mr. Ripley—is accused of embezzling money from a non-profit homeless shelter in conjunction with his volunteering to do the accounting for free. The prosecuting attorney is making her final summation to the jury:

"The defendant," she says as she points an accusing finger at him: "had the motive to carry out this despicable crime: His business was losing money, he was in debt up to his eyeballs, and the bank was about to foreclose on his house. He had the opportunity to carry out this crime: He was the only one with access to the homeless shelter's bank accounts and accounting records. And he had the means: As an expert in accounting and banking, he knew how to skim money from the accounts without drawing attention. In short, you must find Mr. Ripley guilty if you agree that he had the motive, the opportunity, and the means to carry out the crime."

As you can see, in criminal cases, prosecutors attempt to establish guilt by showing that the accused had *motive* — a reason to commit the crime; *opportunity* — a chance to carry out the crime; and *means* — the skills needed to carry out the crime. The search for motive, opportunity, and means (or MOM for short) is at the heart of many crime dramas, and seems to work well in the search for prosecutorial success.

The Search for Academic Success

In this book, I would like to suggest that the same motive-opportunity-means (MOM) approach can apply to your search for academic success. In order to be a successful learner, you need to have:

motive — i.e., reasons to want to learn the material,
opportunity — i.e., conditions conductive to learning the material,
means — i.e., learning strategies that enable you to be an effective learner.

The main theme of this book is that you can become a successful student if you always remember MOM.

In terms of motive, some of the key ingredients for being a successful student are interest and value — i.e., having interest and finding personal value in the material; goals — i.e., wanting to make sense of the material; beliefs — i.e., believing that you can learn the material if you exert enough effort; and response to threats — not allowing stereotypes to destroy your belief in yourself as a learner. In short, the first step in becoming a successful student is to establish your motive for learning. I explore the components of motive in Part 1 of this book.

In terms of opportunity, some of the key ingredients for being a successful student are time—i.e., allocating sufficient time to productively study the material and arranging to use your study time efficiently; place—i.e., creating a place where you can study free of distractions and interruptions; and mind—i.e., creating a focused mental state free of anxiety and mind wandering. In short, the next step in becoming a successful student is to create the conditions needed for your academic learning. I explore the components of opportunity in Part 2 of this book.

In terms of means, recent research has established an impressive assortment of learning strategies that have been shown to improve academic learning. Learning strategies are activities you engage in during learning that are intended to improve your learning. These include rereading confusing text, highlighting important text, learning the key terms, summarizing the material in your own words, outlining or making diagrams to depict the organization of the material, making drawings that depict the structures or processes in the text, testing yourself on the material you just studied, explaining the material to yourself, explaining the material to others, and acting out aspects of the material. In short, the third step in becoming a successful student is to come to the learning situation with the means to learn the material deeply—i.e., with an array of effective learning strategies that you know how and when to use. I explore effective learning strategies in Part 3 of this book.

In short, my goal for you in this book is to help you remember MOM whenever you want to learn. I want you to have the motive, opportunity, and means to succeed. To help you see what I mean, I have devised a collection of scenarios in which students demonstrate how to and how not to establish motive, opportunity, and means. My hope is that by meeting students with effective and ineffective student habits, you will decide to work on establishing some effective ones.

Learning to Learn

No one sets out to be an unsuccessful student. But in any classroom there are students who have developed ineffective study habits over the years—habits that prevent them from achieving the high level of academic success they are capable of achieving. I explore some of these ineffective habits in the chapters of this book, along with recommendations for how to develop effective ones.

What is the reason for students developing ineffective study habits? The reason could be that no one ever took the time to show them how to learn. We, as instructors and students, tend to focus on what to learn, but we rarely focus on how to learn. As I mentioned in the Preface, some educational researchers argue that learning to learn is part of what can be called the *hidden curriculum*—we expect students to learn how to learn but we rarely teach them how to learn. Highly successful learners may have figured out how to learn on their own, or maybe someone gave them some guidance along the way, but for most of us, learning to learn is not a central part of the curriculum. In the following chapters, I take a step in addressing this problem by showing you the central ingredients in learning how to learn, based on scientific evidence from the science of learning.

If you want to develop effective study habits that are intended to help maximize your academic success, then the following 20 chapters of this book are for you. Each chapter introduces you to one of my 20 favorite evidence-based habits of successful learners. Each chapter includes a scenario, an exercise for you to try, a description of the study habit, and a brief summary of what you can do to apply the study habit to your own studying.

Part 1
Motive to Learn

Successful Habit #1

Find Personal Value in What You Are Learning

Biology Blues

Bob is not a big fan of biology. Don't get me wrong, he has his favorite things to do in life. He loves sports, playing action video games, and in school, his favorite subjects are art and music. But he is now taking a course in biology that leaves him absolutely cold. This week's assignment involves reading a chapter that explains how the human body works, including how the digestive system works, how the heart and lungs work, how the immune system works, and how the eyes and ears work. As Bob looks over the chapter he is overcome with an impending sense of boredom. Bob's plan is to sit down somewhere and just power through this awful task of reading a biology chapter. In short, his plan is to not get emotionally involved with the task—just get it over with.

Interest and Value in Learning

What is wrong with Bob's approach to his unpleasant task of reading a biology chapter? On the surface, he seems to be taking a level-headed approach. He doesn't really like the prospect of having to read the material, but he is taking charge and committing himself to just gutting it out like he does for other unappealing tasks.

As I look over this situation, I am concerned that Bob is acting like an unsuccessful student. The problem with Bob's approach is that more than a century's worth of research on interest in learning shows that people learn better when they are personally interested in the material they are studying, and when they see value in the material for their own lives. In short, people work harder to understand the material when they can find personal meaning in what they are learning.

Before he begins the reading task, Bob needs to take a moment to consider why the lesson might be useful to him. If you were Bob's friend, how would you help him see the value in what he is learning? Please place a check mark next to the ideas that you should share with Bob:

☐ A. Tell him to think about how good it will feel to finish this task and be able to cross it off his to-do list.

☐ B. Tell him not to get emotionally involved with material—it is just something he needs to cram into his head for the test.

☐ C. Point out that music, which he loves, depends on how the human ear works, and art, which he loves, depends on how the human eye works, so learning about the biology of hearing and seeing could be useful to him as a musician and artist.

☐ D. Point out that he has serious allergies so understanding how the immune system works might give
him insight into his allergies, and even help him
reduce their intensity.

☐ E. Point out (in a tactful way) that he is a bit over-
weight, so understanding how the human digestive
system works might be helpful to him.

☐ F. Point out that he loves sports, so he might be interested in how the human body increases the rate of
blood flow when athletes exert themselves.

Option A may seem like reasonable tough-love advice.
Some things in life are unpleasant but just need to be done.
But, this approach violates our goal of helping Bob find
a reason to be interested in the material. By telling him
to just get it over with, we would be confirming Bob's
assessment that the material has little value or meaning
for him. I have a similar objection to option B. However,
if you checked options C, D, E, or F, you are on the right
track in helping Bob find value in what he is studying. In
each case, you are helping Bob relate the material with
something in his life that he values, although you might
want to be gentle with option E, as his weight could be
a sore point for him. In short, options C, D, E, and F
reflect the motivational habits of successful students.

Value Habit

You have just learned an important lesson about motivating someone (including yourself) to learn: *People learn*

better when they value and are personally interested in what they learn. We can call this the *value habit*, and it is an excellent place to start on your journey toward becoming a successful student. Try to take a moment to determine why the material you are learning might have some value to you. As the famous educational scholar John Dewey (1913) observed more than 100 years ago in his classic little book, *Interest and Effort in Education*: "If we can secure interest in a given set of facts or ideas we may be perfectly sure that the pupil will direct his energies toward mastering them." Since then, researchers have compiled convincing evidence, particularly in the last few decades, that students learn more deeply when they are interested in the material than when they are not (Alexander & Grossnickle, 2017; Renninger & Hidi, 2016; Wigfield, Tonks, & Klauda, 2016).

So What Should I Do?

Here are some ways to develop the value habit:

1. Look through the chapter or lecture notes and generate a written list of the three most interesting parts along with a sentence telling why each is of interest to you.
2. Write a one-paragraph essay on why this chapter or lecture could be useful to you.
3. Write a one-paragraph introduction to the chapter as if you were the author (or a one-paragraph introduction to the lecture as if you were the instructor) explaining why this material is valuable and interesting.

If none of these tactics appeals to you, you may need to develop your own way of carrying out the value habit. In building your specific tactics, you should be guided by the general strategy summarized in the box.

BOX 1 How to Apply the Value Habit	
Do this:	**Not this:**
Take a moment to find something of personal value or interest to you in the material.	Power through the material even if it is boring to you.

Sources

Alexander, P. A., & Grossnickle, E. M. (2017). Positioning interest and curiosity within a model of academic development. In K. R. Wentzel & D. B. Miele (Eds.), *Handbook of motivation at school* (2nd ed; pp. 188–208). New York: Routledge.

Dewey, J. (1913). *Interest and effort in education.* Boston: Houghton Mifflin Company.

Renninger, K. A., & Hidi, S. E. (2016). *The power of interest for motivation and engagement.* New York: Routledge.

Wigfield, A., Tonks, S. M., & Klauda, S. L. (2016). Expectancy-value theory. In K. R. Wentzel & D. B. Miele (Eds.), *Handbook of motivation at school* (2nd ed; pp. 55–74). New York: Routledge.

Successful Habit #2

Set Your Goal to Mastering the Material

Last Words

The last thing that Kathy's dad said when she set off to college was, "We're spending a lot of money on your college education, so don't flunk out." Those words are ringing through her head as she sits down to study for her first exam in Introduction to Economics, which turns out to be chock full of complicated terms, long equations, and incomprehensible concepts. To make matters worse, she thinks back to class discussions where her classmates seemed to already know the material quite well. Faced with the daunting task of studying her textbook and notes, she has set a goal for herself. She even has written it on an index card that she keeps as a bookmark: "DON'T GET THE LOWEST GRADE IN THE CLASS."

Goals for Learning

Before we analyze this situation, let me ask you to place a check mark next to each kind of goal that you think would be helpful to Kathy to have:

☐ A. I want to avoid looking bad by getting a lower grade than others in the class.

☐ B. I want to look good by getting a higher grade than others in the class.

☐ C. I want to completely understand the material to my satisfaction.

If you chose option A, you are taking Kathy's approach to setting academic goals. You might look at Kathy's situation and think: "Well, at least Kathy is motivated to study. She has a goal that will keep her going." However, when I look at this situation, I suspect she is on the way to becoming an unsuccessful student. Option A reflects what can be called a *performance-avoidance goal*, in which your goal is to avoid poor performance. The problem with this approach is that research shows that academic goals based on avoiding poor performance are not generally associated with academic success (Martin, 2013; Murayama, Elliot, & Friedman, 2012; Senko, 2016). When you seek to avoid poor grades, you are encouraging yourself to learn in a way that is not likely to give you a solid knowledge base to support future learning; instead, you are focused solely on short-term techniques to avoid getting a bad external assessment.

What else could Kathy do? If you chose option B, your focus is also on grades as with option A, but in this case your goal is to achieve good academic performance— that is, you want to look better than others in the class. This might seem like the perfect alternative for Kathy's poor choice, but while I agree that option B is better than option A, it might not be as perfect as it looks. Option B reflects what can be called a *performance-approach goal* in which your goal is to achieve good performance, such as to get better grades than your classmates. In this case, Kathy would work to do well on a test, but may not care about learning the material for the long run. Even worse, if Kathy opts for option B, she runs the risk of becoming a "grade grubber"—someone who wants an A so badly that she will choose classes and instructors solely based on how it affects her GPA (grade point average), will argue with the instructor to get more points on exams even when she doesn't deserve them, and will constantly ask, "Will that be on the test?" For a grade grubber the prize is getting an A for its own sake rather than learning something. Even if Kathy does not fall into the role of a grade grubber, the problem with option B—by itself— is that it does not necessarily involve trying to deeply understand the material so it might not provide a solid basis for future learning. Option B is not necessarily a terrible approach because research shows that seeking to get better grades is linked with academic success in the short term (Martin, 2013; Murayama, Elliot, & Friedman, 2012; Senko, 2016). Certainly, I must admit that grades can be important for opening up future opportunities, and you should be careful to give yourself the best opportunity to achieve the grades you want. However, a focus solely on option B may not be the perfect approach because it does not lead to a long-term commitment to continue learning in the subject area.

If you chose option C, perhaps along with option B, you are on the road to becoming a successful student. Option C reflects what can be called a *mastery goal*, in which you seek to understand the material, that is, you engage in learning for its own sake because you want to make sense out of the material. Research shows that this approach is linked to long-term success and persistence in a field of study (Martin, 2013; Murayama, Elliot, & Friedman, 2012; Senko, 2016). When you combine a *mastery goal* with *a performance-approach* goal, you can combine good grades in the short term with persistence in learning over the long term. In short, mastery goals can give you the foundation you need for future learning and the motivation you need to stick with your academic career when things start to get tough.

Goal Habit

Kathy's situation demonstrates the important point that your academic goals are related to your academic achievement. In short, the *goal habit* is: *People learn better when their goal is to master the material they are studying.* When you are faced with new material to learn, set your sites on completely understanding it. You want to make sense out of the material for the long run, not just memorize it for the sake of doing well on a test and then forget it. For example, this means you need to be on the lookout for parts that need to be clarified so you can seek out the needed clarification. This also means that you need to set specific learning objectives for yourself, and test yourself to make sure you meet them. Additionally, it means that you need to elaborate on the material and connect it with related material you already know. I explore these and related learning strategies in Part 3 on MEANS.

Although researchers have not quite reached consensus on the role of performance-approach goals (Martin, 2013; Murayama, Elliot, & Friedman, 2012; Senko, 2016), it probably makes sense to expand the goal principle to include having a goal of high academic performance. In short, wanting good grades works best as a goal when it is combined with the goal of wanting to understand the material. In contrast, having a performance-approach goal without also having a mastery goal along with it has the potential to lead you down the path to becoming an unsuccessful student because it can leave you with a superficial base of knowledge for future learning and without the motivation to continue your studies.

Unsuccessful students focus exclusively on grades by wanting to avoid getting worse grades than others, or solely wanting to get better grades than others (or even perform as well as others by doing less work). If you want to become a successful student who persists in learning for the long term over your academic career and beyond, then you should approach your learning tasks with a mastery goal of wanting to make sense out of the material. Adding a goal of doing well on grades or external assessments is also associated with academic success, but you should apply this performance-approach goal in conjunction with your mastery goal rather than instead of it.

So What Should I Do?

In order to implement the goal habit, I recommend that you consider some tactics like these:

1. Write down your learning objectives for a lesson.
2. As you study, cross out the objectives you have mastered and circle the ones that need more work.
3. Coordinate your system with some of the ten learning strategies in the MEANS section of this book.

These tactics are intended to keep you focused on the general goal of mastering the material, as summarized in the box.

Box 2: How to Apply the Goal Habit	
Do this:	**Not this:**
Take a moment to clarify what you want to learn from the lesson you are studying, and work hard to learn it.	Study just enough so your grade will not look bad.

Sources

Martin, A. J. (2013). Goal orientation. In J. Hattie & E. M. Anderman (Eds.), *International guide to student achievement* (pp. 353–355). New York: Routledge.

Murayama, K., Elliot, A. J., & Friedman, R. (2012). Achievement goals. In R. M. Ryan (Ed.), *The Oxford handbook of human motivation* (pp. 191–207). New York: Oxford University Press.

Senko, C. (2016). Achievement goal theory: A story of early promises, eventual discords, and future possibilities. In K. R. Wentzel & D. B. Miele (Eds.), *Handbook of motivation at school* (2nd ed; pp. 75–95). New York: Routledge.

Successful Habit #3

Believe that You Can Learn if You Try Hard Enough

Mindy's Math Motto

As part of the requirements for her major, Mindy is required to enroll in the dreaded course Introduction to Statistics, which is scheduled to begin this week. All through high school, Mindy avoided taking higher-level math classes because in her words, "I am just not good in math." She even developed a math motto: "I don't hate math, math hates me." Now, what is she supposed to do? She tried to convince her school counselor that she should not have to take the course at all, especially since she certainly will not take additional optional courses in statistics. Faced with being forced to take this daunting statistics course, Mindy figures she will just sit through class and read the book, without spending too much time on it. She has convinced herself that no matter how hard she works in the course, she will not do very well so she should use her limited time to study for other courses that she can excel at. After all, statistics is just one course she has to take, so she will just focus on working hard in other courses for which she is better suited.

Beliefs for Learning

At first glance, Mindy's plan might seem quite reasonable to you. Maybe you can accept her argument that her time is limited and putting time in studying hard for the statistics class would be wasteful, so her time is better spent on other courses that she can actually do well in. It's all a matter of efficient use of limited time—stick with what you are good at and avoid what you are bad at. That may appear to be a reasonable argument, but in this section I want to show you the pitfalls of Mindy's approach to student-hood. It all comes down to the idea that your beliefs are related to your academic success.

Before we analyze Mindy's plan, let me ask you to place a check mark next to the statements you agree with.

☐ A. Mindy's grade in statistics depends mainly on her mathematical ability.

☐ B. Mindy's grade in statistics depends mainly on how much effort she puts into studying.

☐ C. If Mindy tries hard, she will actually be able to learn the material in her statistics course.

☐ D. No matter how hard she tries, Mindy is not likely to do very well in her statistics course.

☐ E. If Mindy fails the first exam in statistics, that is because she didn't study hard enough.

☐ F. If Mindy fails the first exam in statistics, that is because of her low math ability.

Mindy's study plan is based on her beliefs about her competence to learn statistics. Options A, D, and F reflect aspects of Mindy's beliefs about herself as a statistics student. The way I see it, if you harbor beliefs such as reflected in A, D, or F, you are on your way to becoming an unsuccessful student. Let me explain why.

First, options A and B reflect Mindy's *mindset*—that is, whether she thinks her cognitive ability is fixed or changeable (Dwyer, 2016). A *fixed mindset*—as reflected in option A—is based on the belief that your basic qualities are permanent rather than something that can develop and change. For example, you are either good in math or not, and you can't really alter that. A *growth mindset*—as reflected in option B—is based on the belief that your basic qualities can develop and change through your experience. For example, you can cultivate your skill in math through effort. Research shows that academic success is more likely to come to those who harbor a growth mindset; however, many students have a fixed mindset, which is detrimental to their academic success (Dwyer, 2016). A growth mindset motivates students to work hard to learn the material, which results in better learning.

Second, options C and D reflect Mindy's *self-efficacy beliefs*—her beliefs about her capability to accomplish a specific task (Schunk & DiBenedetto, 2016; Schunk &

Usher, 2012). Low self-efficacy—as reflected in option D—is the belief that you lack the capability to do well on a task, such as believing you do not have what it takes to do well in statistics. High self-efficacy—as reflected in option C—is the belief that you are capable of successfully accomplishing a task, such as believing that you can do well in statistics. It is important to note that self-efficacy is your belief about your capability to accomplish a specific task—such as learn introductory statistics—rather than your self-concept in general. Research shows that academic success is related to self-efficacy, with higher self-efficacy related to higher achievement (Schunk & DiBenedetto, 2016; Schunk & Usher, 2012). Someone with high self-efficacy is more likely to try hard to learn a tough concept or persist with a challenging task.

Third, options E and F reflect Mindy's *attributions* about her test performance—whether she thinks her success or failure on a task is due to her ability or her effort (Graham & Taylor, 2016). *Attributions based on ability*—such as exemplified in option F—reflect the belief that academic success or failure depends on one's ability, so the implication is that exerting effort to study will not have any effect. *Attributions based on effort*—as exemplified in option E—reflect the belief that academic success or failure depends on how hard you work, so the implication is that exerting effort to study will have a positive effect. Research shows that effort-based attributions are more productive for students, as they are associated with better academic achievement (Graham &

Taylor, 2016). In short, if you believe your test score in a course depends on how much work you are willing to do (that is, you believe that your effort will pay off), then you will be motived to exert more effort to learn the material.

Belief Habit

Mindy's plan to avoid working hard in statistics is a case study in being an unsuccessful student, because she is letting her unproductive beliefs stop her from exerting the effort needed to learn the material. The moral of her story can be called the *belief habit: People learn better when they believe their mind can grow rather than being unchangeable, when they believe they can accomplish a specific task if they exert effort, and when they believe that failures and successes on academic tasks depend mainly on effort rather than ability.* In short, the path to becoming a successful student starts with thinking hard about your beliefs about yourself as a learner. When it comes to academic success, the most productive belief you can have is: I can learn if I work hard enough. In short, in order to become a successful student, you should see effort as your path to academic success.

So What Should I Do?

In your quest to develop productive beliefs, I suggest you consider tactics like these:

1. Write a brief essay about a time that you worked hard and accomplished a challenging academic goal.
2. Write a brief statement about how you can succeed on this learning task by working hard.
3. Engage in positive self-talk during studying, such as saying "I can do this."
4. Surround yourself with people who also know you can do this, and who encourage you to exert effort.
5. Coordinate your belief habit with appropriate learning habits from Part 3 on MEANS in this book.

Overall, you want to do things that help you see that your number one asset as a student is your willingness to work hard. Coupled with this belief habit, you need a collection of management and learning habits that will help you use your effort most effectively, as discussed in the OPPORTUNITY and MEANS sections of this book. In choosing specific tactics for implementing the belief habit, you should be guided by the general principle in the box.

Box 3: How to Apply the Belief Habit	
Do this:	**Not this:**
Take a moment to clarify your personal views about yourself as a learner, and to consider the powerful role of your personal effort.	Enter the learning task with the idea that how well you learn depends mainly on your ability.

Sources

Dwyer, C. S. (2016). *Mindset: The new psychology of success*. New York: Ballantine Books.

Graham, S., & Taylor, A. Z. (2016). Attribution theory and motivation in school. In K. R. Wentzel & D. B. Miele (Eds.), *Handbook of motivation at school* (2nd ed; pp. 11–33). New York: Routledge.

Schunk, D. H., & DiBenedetto, M. K. (2016). Self-efficacy theory in education. In K. R. Wentzel & D. B. Miele (Eds.), *Handbook of motivation at school* (2nd ed; pp. 34–54). New York: Routledge.

Schunk, D. H., & Usher, E. L. (2012). Social cognitive theory and motivation. In R. M. Ryan (Ed.), *The Oxford handbook of human motivation* (pp. 13–27). New York: Oxford University Press.

Successful Habit #4

Feel Challenged Rather than Threatened

First Day

Karen is taking her first computer science class at her local junior college over the summer. It is the first day of class, and she got to class early to get a good seat in the first row. As the room begins to fill, she looks around without success for a familiar face. She can't help but notice that the room is mostly full of young men, all looking quite ready to dig into the course. She wonders, "Are they better prepared than I am for this course?" There are a few women sprinkled here and there throughout the room, but Karen thinks maybe they look out of place.

The instructor, Mr. Pinkstaff, is standing at the podium, looking over his notes, without so much as a welcoming smile. Karen uses her smartphone to take a quick look at the faculty in the Computer Science Department. Out of 20 faculty members, she sees only two women, and one of them is a temporary instructor. Starting to feel a little queasy, she texts her friend Carol, saying she is sitting in her introductory computer science class. However, Carol does not quite provide the support Karen is looking for, when she writes back: "why would u want to do that?"

Thoughts start running through her head: "Do I belong here?" "Can women succeed in computer science?" "Should I rethink this?"

Her line of reasoning goes like this: Women don't do so well in computer science. I am a woman. Therefore, I probably will not do so well.

Is there something wrong with Karen's logic? Let's see what you think.

Threats to Learning

Clearly, Karen feels a little threatened at this point, before she even starts the course. What should she do about it? Place a check mark next to each move you think she should make:

☐ A. Karen's logic is flawless, so she should quit the course.

☐ B. Women don't do as well in computer science as men, so women like Karen should not expect to excel in computer science courses.

☐ C. Karen should realize that she is likely to perform worse than her classmates no matter what she does, so it probably does not pay for her to exert much effort.

☐ D. Karen should tell herself the idea that women can't excel in computer science is baloney.

☐ E. Karen should see this class as a challenge she can meet, and work hard to do her best.

These options reflect the impact of what can be called *stereotype threat* on Karen's motivation to learn. If you experience *stereotype threat* in an academic setting this means you see yourself as a member of a group that has been characterized as lacking competence (Master, Cheryan, & Meltzoff, 2016; Steele, 2010), such as believing that women are not good in computer science, as reflected in those insidious options A, B, and C. Research shows that when students accept negative stereotypes about their group, they may exert less effort to learn and perform more poorly, as reflected in option C (Master, Cheryan, & Meltzoff, 2016; Steele, 2010). They may even engage in *self-handicapping,* in which they make it nearly impossible for themselves to attain academic success (such as "misplacing" their textbook) so they have a ready-made excuse for poor performance. Believing in negative stereotypes about your group can turn you into an unsuccessful student.

In contrast, if you take a stereotype-free approach to learning, as reflected in heroic options D and E, you are more likely to be motivated to learn. If you want to be a successful student, an important step is not to believe in stereotypes when it comes to the power of your effort to improve your learning.

You can counter the destructive power of stereotypes by carefully considering what is wrong in each step of Karen's logic:

1. "Women don't do so well in computer science." The truth of the matter is that women tend to get better grades than men in just about every subject area. When given a chance, women have been highly successful in the field of computer science. So, the first step is to reject this destructive premise.
2. "I am a woman." Certainly this is true for Karen, but she is also an individual who has an excellent background in mathematics and a strong interest in robotics in particular. Thus, the second step is for her to see herself as having what it takes to succeed in computer science.
3. "Therefore, I probably will not do so well." If Karen accepts this statement, she is likely to exert little effort in the course. Instead, a much more productive view for Karen is that she can do well in the course if she works hard.

In an academic learning situation like Karen's, you must choose between two interpretations: You can feel *threatened*, or you can feel *challenged*. If you allow yourself to feel threatened, you are likely to become demotivated, exert less effort, and fulfill the bogus stereotype by performing poorly (Jamieson, 2017). If you feel challenged, you are likely to be motivated, exert more effort, and achieve better academic performance (Jamieson, 2017). In short, to some extent, your interpretation of the situation can influence how hard you try to learn, which can influence your academic performance.

Threat Habit

Research on the destructive power of stereotype threat (Jamieson, 2017; Master, Cheryan, & Meltzoff, 2016; Stelle, 2010) yields the *threat habit: People learn better when they avoid the trap of believing in stereotypes about their ability to learn.* Specifically, people learn better when they feel challenged rather than threatened by a learning task. The appropriate response to a situation like Karen's, or any situation in which you feel bullied, is to view learning the material as a challenge you can meet through your own effort. Your thoughts about yourself as a learner are an important factor contributing to your motivation to learn. Our battle against stereotype threat yields a clear piece of advice: Develop ways to counter ugly stereotypes that cloud your thinking about yourself as a learner; see yourself as a competent learner who can be successful if you work hard.

So What Should I Do?

When you are feeling threatened by a learning task, I suggest that you consider tactics such as the following:

1. If you are questioning your competence, push back and follow some of the suggestions for the belief habit (discussed under Successful Habit #3).

2. If you are feeling anxiety building up, take a deep breath and follow some of the suggestions for the anxiety habit (discussed under Successful Habit #9).
3. If you want to be a stereotype-buster but aren't sure how to do it, roll up your sleeves and check out the ten learning habits (discussed under Successful Habits #11–20).

As you can see the threat habit is a special extension of the belief habit, so you can use some of the same tactics for both of them. Your tactics should be based on the general approach described in the box.

Box 4: How to Apply the Threat Habit

Do this:	**Not this:**
See yourself as a competent learner who can succeed if you work hard enough.	Let others define how good of a learner you are.

Sources

Jamieson, J. P. (2017). Challenge and threat appraisals. In A. J. Elliot, C. S. Dweck, & D. S. Yaeger (Eds.), *Handbook of competence and motivation* (2nd ed; pp. 175–191). New York: Guilford.

Master, A., Cheryan, S., & Meltzoff, A. N. (2016). Motivation and identity. In K. R. Wentzel & D. B. Miele (Eds.), *Handbook of motivation at school* (2nd ed; pp. 300–319). New York: Routledge.

Steele, C. M. (2010). *Whistling Vivaldi and other clues to how stereotypes affect us.* New York: W. W. Norton & Company.

Part 2
Opportunity to Learn

Successful Habit #5

Give Yourself Time to Learn

Fast Eddie

Ed does not like to waste time studying if he doesn't have to. He tries to be efficient with his time. Instead of going to boring lectures, he watches the lectures online on his laptop at home, running them at 2X speed. This way it takes him half the time to listen to the instructor's words of wisdom, although they are so high-pitched they sound a little bit like they are being spoken by a chipmunk. As he listens, he writes down pieces of the instructor's statements word-for-word in his notebook, allocating one or two pages for each lecture. Next, he gives himself one minute per page for reading the textbook, using his handy yellow marker to highlight anything that catches his fancy as he skims along. When it is time to study for an exam, he looks over the notes in his notebook and the underlined material in his textbook. Ed's efficient study style has earned him the nickname of *Fast Eddie* among his friends, but he wears that name as a badge of honor.

Time to Learn

You might look at Ed's approach to coursework and say he is doing a great job. He is spending his time in a very efficient way. He is the epitome of a good student. But when I look at what Ed is doing, I see someone who is on the path to becoming an unsuccessful student.

Let me begin by asking you to put a check mark next to the factors that you think are important for Ed's academic achievement:

☐ A. Highlighting important material in a textbook

☐ B. Copying down important phrases from a lecture

☐ C. Watching videos of lectures rather than actually attending lectures

☐ D. Spending time engaged in productive learning

If you checked A or B, you opted for somewhat ineffective learning strategies. As described in Part 3 on MEANS, research shows these learning strategies are not ideal for fostering deep learning. You can read about them more fully in Part 3 on MEANS. Similarly, option C is not supported by strong research evidence, in spite of the popularity of online courses, including MOOCs (Massive Open Online Courses). Don't get me wrong, learning from video lectures is likely to be just as effective as learning from face-to-face lectures, but it is not likely to improve learning as compared to face-to-face lectures, especially if it is played at double speed. This leaves us with option D as the only one that has been shown to substantially improve learning. The way I see it, Ed is likely to become an unsuccessful student because he chooses options A, B, and C, which are not particularly effective ways to improve learning. Instead, he short-changes himself by not using sufficient time to learn (option D), which has been shown to be an essential ingredient in successful learning (van Gog, 2013). If you want to become a successful student, you should home in on option D—allocating sufficient time to learn.

Time Habit

The case of Fast Eddie highlights the important role of time as a condition for learning. According to the *time habit* (as well as the long-standing *total time hypothesis*): *The more you engage in focused study, the more you learn.* This is one of the fundamental principles of learning dating back more than 100 years to early research by the German psychologist Hermann Ebbinghaus, as reported in his classic 1885 book, *Memory*. Ebbinghaus (1885/1964) read a list of nonsense syllables (each consisting of a consonant followed by a vowel followed by a consonant) and then tried to remember them a day later. The more times he practiced the list, the better he did at remembering the words a day later. In short, he was the first to show that there was a direct, positive relationship between time spent studying and amount remembered on a test.

Since that time, research on academic learning has confirmed that the amount of time spent studying is positively related to test performance in school (Ericsson & Pool, 2016; van Gog, 2013). However, it is important to note that not all forms of practice are equally effective. Research shows that learning time is most productive when you are actively engaged in making sense of the core material, which can be called *engaged learning time* (van Gog, 2013), and when you practice at a high level of challenge with detailed feedback on how you are doing, which can be called *deliberate practice* (Ericsson & Pool, 2016).

In short, based on the time principle, I can recommend that you spend sufficient amounts of time engaged in productive studying. In this section on OPPORTUNITY our focus is on conditions that foster learning. The most fundamental ingredient for having an opportunity to learn something new is that you allocate enough time to learn. Learning takes time. How to use that time productively is the subject of Part 3 on MEANS. When you give yourself time to learn, you are on the path to becoming a successful student.

So What Should I Do?

In support of the time habit, I recommend you consider these kinds of tactics:

1. Set aside time slots on your calendar dedicated to studying specific material.

2. If possible, set aside the same time slots every week so you get used to the rhythm of studying in your schedule.
3. If possible, indicate the specific content you will study for each time slot.
4. Adjust or add to your study schedule as needed.

Time is a precious resource in the world of academic success, so you will want to manage it carefully. Your tactics should be guided by the general strategy summarized in the box.

Box 5: How to Apply the Time Habit	
Do this:	**Not this:**
Plan your schedule to include study time.	Minimize the time you allocate to studying.

Sources

Ebbinghaus, H. (1885/1964). *Memory*. New York: Dover.

Ericsson, A., & Pool, R. (2016). *Peak: Secrets from the science of expertise*. New York: Houghton Mifflin Harcourt.

van Gog, T. (2013). Time on task. In J. Hattie & E. M. Anderman (Eds.), *International guide to student achievement* (pp. 432–433). New York: Routledge.

Space Out Your Study Time Across Several Sessions

Midterm Madness

Maddie's calculus exam is scheduled for Monday. It covers four chapters and eight corresponding lectures. Maddie has read the book and attended the lectures but she has not done any preparation beyond that. She plans to devote every waking minute on Sunday to studying for the exam—or more realistically, a total of four hours for sure. When Sunday rolls around, she works from about 8:00 pm to midnight, studying her class notes and the material she highlighted in the textbook chapters. Exhausted after four hours of studying, she goes to bed thinking she has done a successful job of preparing for the exam.

Spacing of Time for Learning

Maddie's approach to her midterm exam is to go out with a bang—allocate all her study time to one big effort, preferably right before the day of the exam. You might think this is a reasonable approach. Just to make sure, please check the statements below that make sense to you.

☐ A. It is best to study all at one time for an exam so you don't have to waste time getting back up to speed from where you left off.

☐ B. It is best to study right before the exam in order to minimize forgetting.

☐ C. Spaced practice is more effective than massed practice.

☐ D. Completing assignments right before the deadline is the hallmark of poorly performing students.

Maddie's approach involves what has been called, *massed practice,* which involves carrying out your learning all at once or in concentrated periods (such as one four-hour session in Maddie's case). An alternative approach is what can be called, *spaced practice,* which involves breaking up the available learning time into shorter time periods that are distributed over time (such as a one-hour session every day for four days in Maddie's case). There is strong research support, dating back more than 100 years, for the spacing effect (Brown, Roediger, & McDaniel, 2014; Dunlosky, Rawson, Marsh, Nathan & Willingham, 2013; Ebbinghaus, 1885/1964; Mayer, 2011): You will learn more if you spread out your studying over time rather than studying for the same amount of time in a single session. In short, the consensus among researchers in the science of learning is that spaced practice is more effective than massed practice (Brown, Roediger, & McDaniel, 2014; Dunlosky,

Rawson, Marsh, Nathan & Willingham, 2013; Ebbinghaus, 1885/1964; Mayer, 2011). As you can see, Maddie's study plan violates this research-based advice, and reflects the study habit of an unsuccessful student. In contrast, if you want to take an evidence-based approach to successful studying, you should not check option A and you should check option C.

Why does spaced practice work better than massed practice? One explanation is that you lose interest in studying at a high level of intensity when you have to repeatedly study the same material in one session. A related explanation is that when you space out practice, each time you study the same material you are creating new ways to find it in your memory, but with massed practice you are storing and retrieving the material the same way.

A second element in Maddie's approach is to study right before the deadline rather than well in advance of the deadline, as reflected in option B. Maddie says that she forgets everything within a day so it makes sense to cram right before the exam rather than days or weeks in advance. On the surface, it appears that she has support from classic research showing that forgetting occurs quite rapidly for memorized material, with most of the forgetting occurring within one day. However, if you look closer at that classic research, you will see that a great deal of forgetting of memorized material occurs even within one hour, so you can conclude that cramming may not be a very practical approach.

A much more successful approach is to use study techniques that involve more than rote memorization, such as are described in Part 3 on MEANS, which have been shown to last much longer and even shine better on delayed tests after a week or more. For example, a recent study found that engineering students who completed their homework assignments within one day of the deadline earned lower grades in the class than those who completed their homework assignments well in advance of the deadline (Rawson, Stahovich, & Mayer, 2017). This is why cramming turns out to be an unsuccessful study habit, and why I was hoping you would check option D.

Spacing Habit

What can we learn from the problems with Maddie's plan to "go out with a bang"? She should have spaced out her study time rather than concentrating it all in one glorious cram session the day before the test. A look at her unsuccessful study habits helps demonstrate the merits of the *spacing habit: People learn better when they allocate their study time across multiple shorter sessions spread out over time rather than when they allocate that same amount of study time to one long session.* Unfortunately, research shows that students are not aware of the benefits of spaced practice as a successful study habit, and in some cases even rate their learning as higher with massed practice (Brown, Roediger, & McDaniel, 2014; Dunlosky, Rawson, Marsh, Nathan, & Willingham, 2013). Similarly, research shows that students tend to concentrate their study time as the test date approaches (Rawson, Stahovich, & Mayer, 2017). It might be hard for you to shed your unsuccessful habits about spacing (and cramming), but there is overwhelming evidence that your performance will improve if you follow this simple recommendation for successful studying: Allocate sufficient time to studying and carefully spread it out across several days rather than concentrating it all on the day before the exam.

So What Should I Do?

Here are some specific ways to implement the spacing habit:

1. On your calendar, plan out many study sessions that span the entire term.
2. For any given course, schedule several regular time slots every week that cover the entire term. Perhaps color code the time slots or portions of time slots so each course gets a different color.
3. For each course, if possible, briefly indicate what and how you plan to study during each time slot. Keep track of your progress on each study goal.
4. Adjust your schedule as needed, including adding extra time in the weeks before the exam if needed.

Your overall goal is to make sure you have spread out many opportunities to study over the term rather than scheduling one long study session right before the exam, as summarized in the box.

BOX 6	How to Apply the Spacing Habit
Do this:	**Not this:**
Plan your schedule to space out many study sessions.	Cram all your studying into one long session the day before the test.

Sources

Brown, P. C., Roediger, H. L., & McDaniel, M. A. (2014). *Make it stick: The science of successful learning.* Cambridge, MA: Harvard University Press.

Dunlosky, J., Rawson, K. A., Marsh, E. J., Nathan, M. J., & Willingham, D. T. (2013). Improving students' learning with effective techniques: Promising directions from cognitive and educational psychology. *Psychological Science in the Public Interest, 14*(1), 4–58.

Ebbinghaus, H. (1885/1964). *Memory.* New York: Dover.

Mayer, R. E. (2011). *Applying the science of learning.* Boston: Pearson.

Rawson, K., Stahovich, T. F., & Mayer, R. E. (2017). Homework and achievement: Using smartpen technology to find the connection. *Journal of Educational Psychology, 109*, 208–219.

Alternate Among a Few Different Things in Each Session

Stacy Studies Statistics

Stacy is preparing for a quiz in her statistics class. The quiz covers three kinds of statistical tests—*t-tests* for comparing whether the means of two groups are different (such as whether the students in Mr. A's class get significantly better or worse grades on the final exam than students in Ms. B's class), *chi-square tests* for comparing whether two groups differ in the proportions of some category (such as whether the proportion of girls and boys in Mr. A's class is significantly different than the proportion of boys and girls in Ms. B's class), and *correlations* for determining the relationship between two variables (such as determining whether student height in inches is significantly related to their grade on the final exam in Mr. A's class).

Stacy dutifully blocks out three one-hour periods of time to study in her schedule. In the first session, she reads up on t-tests and practices solving a set of t-test word problems, looking up the correct answer after she completes each problem. In the second session, she does the same for chi-square, and in the third session she does the same for correlation. She is proud of herself for following her study schedule and is confident she will do well on the quiz. She has learned to solve t-test, chi-square, and correlation problems by using the corresponding formula to compute an answer.

Sitting in class on quiz day, she is all smiles and ready for the quiz. However, when she gets her quiz booklet, a sense of confusion overcomes her. It contains problems to solve, each on its own page. As she stares at the first problem, Stacy realizes that although she knows how to compute answers based on the formula for each type of statistical test, she is not sure which type of problem she is looking at. When she studied, all of the problems were the same type so all she had to do was apply the formula, but now on the quiz the three types of problems are mixed together and she does not know what to do.

Interleaving for Learning

Stacy has a problem with study time. On the bright side, she did the right thing by scheduling time to study. However, she blocked her studying so that she covered just one topic in each session. Tell me what you think about the way she organized that time by placing a check mark next to the items you endorse:

☐ A. Blocked practice is best because you can master one thing before moving on to the next.

☐ B. Blocked practice is best because you get concentrated practice on solving each type of problem.

☐ C. Blocked practice is not best because it taught Stacy what to do but not when to do it.

If you agree with options A and B, you support Stacy's decision to organize her study time into blocks, with each block focusing on one to-be-learned topic. However, that approach had poor consequences for Stacy, as is reflected in option C.

Let's consider two ways to organize your study time. If you have a certain amount of study time to study several topics you can organize your time in two ways:

> *Blocked practice* involves completely studying one topic before moving on to the next one.
> *Interleaved practice* involves mixing the topics together and alternating among them.

As reflected in Stacy's trouble with the quiz, research shows that in some situations, blocked practice turns out to be an unsuccessful study habit (Brown, Roediger, & McDaniel, 2014; Dunlosky, Rawson, Marsh, Nathan & Willingham, 2013). It sounds like a good idea to master one topic before moving on to the next, but when you will have to solve problems out of context, blocked practice can leave you confused, as was the case for Stacy. If Stacy used interleaved practice, she would use the first session to briefly read up on all three tests, and then try to solve a set of problems that contained all three types. She would do the same thing in the second and third sessions.

There is a small but growing research base showing that under appropriate circumstances interleaved practice is more effective than blocked practice (Brown, Roediger, & McDaniel, 2014; Dunlosky, Rawson, Marsh, Nathan & Willingham, 2013). Part of the reason may be that interleaved practice forces you to space out your studying—such as studying each of three problem types a little bit on three different sessions rather than a lot in one session (consistent with Successful Habit #6). It also helps you learn to recognize the features that allow you to distinguish among problem types so you know both what to do and when to do it.

Consider a situation in an art history class, where you need to learn to recognize the paintings of each of ten great artists. Suppose there are ten paintings for each artist with the artist's name below each one. In blocked practice, you would study all ten paintings by artist #1 before seeing all ten paintings by artist #2, and so on. In interleaved practice you would see ten paintings in the first set, one from each artist, and so on for each set of ten paintings. Research shows that interleaved practice results in better learning of which paintings go with which artists (Kornell & Bjork, 2008). One explanation is that interleaved practice helps you learn distinctive features that allow you to discriminate one artist (or problem type) from another.

Interleaving Habit

As we have seen, when you block your study time you may be on the road to becoming an unsuccessful student, at least in some situations. Alternatively, when you interleave your study time, you are acting like a successful student. What we learned from this example can be called the *interleaving habit: People learn better when they study different kinds of problems or topics mixed together in each of several sessions rather than separately with each problem or topic in its own session.* Generally, students perform better during learning with blocked practice, leaving students with a stronger feeling that they know the material, but on tests given after learning, students tend to perform better with interleaved practice (Kornell & Bjork, 2008). This suggests that you cannot let an inaccurate feeling of knowing the material dictate which approach you use to organize your study time. Although the benefits of interleaving do not come through in all studies, there is enough evidence to be confident in giving you this simple advice: When you have set aside time to study several different problems or topics, mix them together (or repeatedly alternate among them) rather than trying to master each problem or topic separately.

So What Should I Do?

Once you have sprinkled some study time slots on your calendar, you can refine them so that you alternate among the topics you are studying, such as using the following tactics:

1. For each study slot, list at least two or three different study tasks so you can alternate among them. For example, first outline a section of a lesson, then give yourself a mini-lecture on the material, and go over flash cards covering the key terms; then repeat that for the next section, and so on. In this way, you can alternative among study activities.
2. If you have a long time slot, alternate your studying among different courses. Maybe list that you will first read material from course X and then from course Y, and then go back to read material from course X followed by course Y, and so on.

The box below gives you the general principle to guide your selection of specific tactics for exercising the interleaving habit.

BOX 7 How to Apply the Interleaving Habit

Do this:	Not this:
Plan your schedule to alternate among topics and study activities in each session.	Plan your schedule so you have one long uninterrupted period for each topic.

Sources

Brown, P. C., Roediger, H. L., & McDaniel, M. A. (2014). *Make it stick: The science of successful learning.* Cambridge, MA: Harvard University Press.

Dunlosky, J., Rawson, K. A., Marsh, E. J., Nathan, M. J., & Willingham, D. T. (2013). Improving students' learning with effective techniques: Promising directions from cognitive and educational psychology. *Psychological Science in the Public Interest, 14*(1), 4–58.

Kornell, N., & Bjork, R. A. (2008). Learning concepts and categories: Is spacing the "enemy of induction"? *Psychological Science, 19*, 585–592.

Successful Habit #8

Study in a Distraction-Free Zone

A Spoonful of Music and Other Myths

Sal has a date with his philosophy textbook. He has scoped out a comfortable chair, brought his textbook and highlighter in his backpack, and allocated 20 minutes to cuddle up and read an assigned chapter in his philosophy textbook. The material is quite dry, so to spice it up he also decided to bring along his earbuds and iPad so he can rock out (at low volume, of course) to a new indie band he likes as he reads. His plan is that the pace of the music will keep him plowing through the chapter, no matter how boring the material is. The way Sal sees it, listening to that music while reading the chapter is like adding a spoonful of sugar to help the medicine go down.

Amanda is sitting in her usual seat in the tenth row of a large lecture class on introduction to astronomy, with her printed-out PowerPoint slides and her iPhone on her desk. The instructor is going through a seemingly endless collection of PowerPoint slides, each with headings and bullet points that Amanda compares to the printed-out version she brought to class. Along the way she sends off a quick text to a friend about plans for later in the day, and gets into a back-and-forth texting conversation. She feels she is perfectly able to follow the instructor's lecture at the same time she fires off texts and reads incoming ones. In fact, she is sure texting helps her stay alert.

Ted has to write a one-page essay for his philosophy class and it is due tomorrow. He carries his trusty laptop computer to the campus coffee shop where he sits at a table with some of his chatty friends. After getting his coffee and chatting for a while, he opens his laptop and gets to work checking out websites for ideas and typing out his masterpiece. Occasionally, he asks his friends a question and even adds to the ongoing conversation at the table; then, he gets back to working on his paper. There are also multiple TV screens around the room, and he looks up from time to time to see the latest news scrolling along on one of the screens, and especially to follow a basketball game on another screen. According to Ted, these mini-breaks refresh his brain; and sitting with his friends and being surrounded by TV screens puts him in a good mood for writing.

What do all three of these scenarios have in common? In each scenario, a student is engaged in multitasking while working on academic learning. In each scenario, the student has a good reason to multitask—Sal listens to music while reading to keep a steady pace, Amanda texts during class to keep alert, and Ted completes assignments in a coffee shop surrounded by friends and TV screens that keep him in a good mood. You might say, here are three fine students who have learned to combine somewhat boring academic tasks with more enjoyable environments such as listening to music, texting, and being around friends.

Place for Learning

Are Sal, Amanda, and Ted really the excellent students they think they are? Before I give you my take on these three scenarios, let me ask you to place a check mark next to each of the following statements that you agree with:

☐ A. Young people today have been brought up in the digital age, so they are able to use technology to multitask without harming their performance.

☐ B. Reading with music playing in your ears is a good way to learn.

☐ C. Texting during a lecture class can be done in ways that keep you more alert for learning.

☐ D. Doing academic work in a coffee shop with friends and commotion helps you stay in a good mood for learning.

☐ E. Anything that distracts you from reading, listening, and writing is harmful to your learning.

☐ F. Your mind can process only a limited amount of
material at any one time, so if you are focusing on
extraneous tasks this will distract you from your
learning.

If you checked option A, you subscribe to a popular
view that is espoused by some visionaries in the field
of technology. In contrast, scholars who take a scientific approach can't find evidence to support the opinion expressed in option A. Specifically, Jeffrey Holmes
in his little book, *Great Myths of Education and Learning*, describes research showing that the claim that multitasking does not inhibit academic performance is a
myth (Holmes, 2016). For example, students who have
the most experience in using multiple technologies at the
same time—such as texting, reading Facebook posts, and
talking on the phone all at the same time—tend to do
the worst on cognitive tests of multitasking. In addition,
when students are asked to send and receive texts during
a lecture, they learn less than when they listen to a lecture
in a cell-phone-free context. In short, multitasking is an
approach that leads to becoming an unsuccessful student.
You can put yourself on the road to academic success by
rejecting the multitasking myth.

Similarly, if you checked options B, C, and/or D, perhaps in sympathy with Sal, Amanda, or Ted, you are also
on the path to becoming an unsuccessful student. To my
way of thinking, the students described in this chapter
are displaying the habits of unsuccessful students. They

are filling their heads with distractions that limit the amount of processing capacity left over for deep learning. By switching back and forth between academic and non-academic tasks, they limit their opportunity to process the academic material and are more likely to deal with it at a superficial level, if at all. In short, distracted learning can be as detrimental to your academic success as distracted driving can be detrimental to your survival on the road.

In contrast, if you checked options E and/or F you are rejecting the unsuccessful approach to being a student and opting for a successful one. Research shows that anything you do that distracts you from your core academic task such as reading, listening, or writing, can take away from the cognitive capacity you have available for engaging in deep learning (Brown & Kaminske, 2018; Holmes, 2016; Mayer, 2011). Deep learning requires that you have cognitive capacity for figuring out what is important, mentally organizing the material, and integrating it with relevant knowledge from long-term memory (Mayer, 2011). A central discovery in cognitive science is that humans have a very limited working memory capacity, which allows us to process only a few items at any one time (Mayer, 2011). Therefore, if you are engaged in *extraneous cognitive processing*—that is, cognitive processing that does not support your learning—you are taking away cognitive capacity that could have been used for *generative cognitive processing*—that is, cognitive processing aimed at making sense of the to-be-learned material, such as described in the Part 3 on MEANS. When you take away cognitive capacity that could have been used for learning the task at hand, it is like building something with one hand tied behind your back.

Multitasking Habit

The multitasking trio described in this chapter help to highlight the importance of learning in a *distraction-free zone*—a place where you can devote all of your attention to the learning task without having to engage in extraneous cognitive processing. According to the *multitasking habit: The less you engage in extraneous activities during learning, the more you learn*. Humans tend to pay attention to one task at a time, so there really is no such thing as multitasking. Instead, people who carry out two (or more) tasks at a time actually are switching back and forth among them. When people engage in extraneous processing during the time they should be listening, reading, or writing in academic tasks, they are handicapping their opportunity to succeed as learners. Unsuccessful students embrace technology-induced distraction, but you can be a successful student if you can figure out how to learn in a distraction-free zone.

So What Should I Do?

In short, based on the multitasking habit, I can recommend that you find a place to study that is free of distractions and interruptions, including technology-induced distractions such as listening to background music while reading, half-monitoring background TV while writing, or engaging in texting, playing a game, or using the Internet while listening to a classroom lecture. Minimizing distractions and interruptions includes finding a place to study that does not have a lot of commotion, noise, and clutter, but is well-lit, comfortable, and has sufficient space for you. You might want to turn off your cell phone and put it out of sight. Here is my list of suggested tactics for finding or creating a place to study that minimizes external distractions:

1. Turn off loud music, video, or television screens while you read or study.
2. Turn off your access to the Internet while you are listening to a lecture.
3. Turn off your phone and notifications of messages while you read, study, or attend a lecture. In fact, keep your personal devices out of sight.
4. Grab a comfortable spot with adequate lighting, but without ambient commotion, clutter, or conversation.

When it comes to the opportunity to learn, an important ingredient for successful studying is a distraction-free place to learn. Learning requires your full attention to process the material. How best to use your cognitive processing during learning is the subject of Part 3 on MEANS. When you give yourself a place to learn, you are clearing the way to becoming a successful student, as summarized in the box.

BOX 8 How to Apply the Multitasking Habit

Do this:	Not this:
Find or create a place that is free of distractions and interruptions.	Accompany your studying with background multitasking activities you like, such as listening to music, text messaging, and watching videos.

Sources

Brown, A. M., & Kaminske, A. N. (2018). *Five teaching and learning myths debunked.* New York: Routledge.

Holmes, J. D. (2016). *Great myths of education and learning.* Malden, MA: Wiley Blackwell.

Mayer, R. E. (2011). *Applying the science of learning.* Boston: Pearson.

Successful Habit #9

Clear Your Mind of Worries

A World of Worry

Marga is sitting in her introductory calculus course, with her notebook open, ready to take notes on today's lecture. With a warm smile and friendly voice, the instructor begins by saying: "Hello everyone." Marga takes a deep breath and hopes that the lecture will continue with more soothing words. The instructor begins by working out an example problem on the board, explaining each step as she writes. But when Marga sees those math symbols on the board she feels her body starting to tense up, and soon a sense of nervousness and fear overtakes her from head to toe. Her mind goes blank as negative thoughts and worries overtake her mind. She feels frozen with fear and is unable to take useful notes, or even follow what the instructor is saying.

What is happening to Marga? Marga appears to be suffering from *learner anxiety*—an emotional state caused when a learner anticipates negative academic outcomes or other harmful events (Maloney & Beilock, 2012). Marga's reaction reminds us that academic learning has an emotional side to it that can influence academic success.

Test Your Math Anxiety

For example, for each of the following items please rate your feelings of fear, tension, and nervousness, on a scale of 1 to 5 with 1 meaning you have no negative feelings and 5 meaning you have strong negative feelings. Write your number in the slot to the left of each statement.

☐ When you watch a teacher work out a math problem on the board.

☐ When you are given a pop-quiz in a math class.

☐ When you think of a math test that is coming up tomorrow.

☐ When you are called on to answer a question in a math class.

☐ When you are studying for a math test.

These items are adapted from a much longer mathematics anxiety rating scale (Suinn & Winston, 2003). If your total score is 15 or above, you are expressing some symptoms of math anxiety, but to be sure you would need to take a longer survey that has been validated through research studies (Suinn & Winston, 2003). Marga appears to be someone who would score high on such a survey.

Calm for Learning

What should Marga do about her worries? Please place a checkmark next to each statement you endorse:

☐ A. A little bit of worry is a good thing, because it will motivate Marga to work hard. She should let her worries motivate her.

☐ B. Marga needs to feel perfectly calm during academic tasks so she should just ignore her worries and fears.

☐ C. Too much worry is a bad thing, because it can prevent Marga from thinking clearly about learning or performing. She should develop ways to cope with her worries.

As I look at Marga's case, I see someone whose negative emotional state is preventing her from having a clear mind that is ready to learn. When your anxiety about learning diminishes your opportunity to learn, you are becoming an unsuccessful student. Just like physical distractions such as too much multitasking during learning can limit your opportunity to learn, emotional distractions such as overwhelming feelings of anxiety during learning also can limit your opportunity to learn (Maloney & Beilock, 2012).

Let's see how the three possible approaches to Marga's situation work out. Option A seems like a reasonable answer because research shows that a low level of arousal can improve performance. However, you need to be careful in supposing that Marga should "let her worries motivate her" because in her case, her apprehension is overwhelming. A reason option A is problematic is that research in the science of learning shows that our working memory capacity—which we use for learning—is quite limited (Huang & Mayer, 2016). If you are thinking about how worried you are, you may not have sufficient cognitive capacity left to engage in meaningful learning. That is, if your mind is full of negative thoughts, you may not have capacity left to engage in learning processes such as figuring out what is most important, mentally reorganizing the material, and relating it to your relevant prior knowledge activated from your long-term memory. This is why I am apprehensive about the advice to "let your worries motivate you." In Part 1 on MOTIVE, you explored some more effective ways to motivate your learning; excessive worrying was not one of them.

Option B also seems to make sense on the surface, because excessive worrying interferes with learning; but it is flawed, because it is unrealistic to expect Marga to somehow ignore her emotional state while learning. When someone is paralyzed with fear, frozen by tension, or overwhelmed with worry, they are not able to turn it off because someone told them to do so. In short, sometimes it is not possible to completely separate your feelings from your thoughts, so Marga needs to develop ways to combat and cope with her negative thoughts.

Option C is my favorite solution because it recognizes the destructive effects of anxiety on learning, and offers alternatives to asking Marga to "just say no" to her negative thoughts. One research-based approach to helping Marga cope is to offer positive words of support before and throughout the learning process (Huang & Mayer, 2016). Another research-based approach is to allow Marga to vent by expressing her feelings in words, such as writing about how she feels (Huang & Mayer, 2016). Finally, Marga can learn to reframe her interpretation of physiological changes such as increased heartrate as a signal that she should feel challenged rather than threatened as suggested by successful research on biofeedback relaxation training (Aritzeta, Soroa, Balluerka, Muela, Gorostiaga, & Aliri, 2017). We want to limit the amount of cognitive processing that Marga devotes to thinking about how nervous and fearful she feels while she is learning, so she can have a working memory system that is ready to be used for learning.

In short, if you want to be a successful student, having a clear mind that is free from negative thoughts of worry is an important aspect of creating the opportunity to learn.

Anxiety Habit

Marga's situation has shown us that emotional states can affect cognitive states needed for learning. The *anxiety habit* is: *People learn better when their mind is not clouded with negative thoughts of worry.* When you are thinking about how nervous you are, you have less cognitive capacity to be able to make sense of the to-be-learned material. Based on the anxiety habit,

I can recommend that you confront any anxiety you are feeling and work out ways to cope with it before you start the task of learning. One way to manage your feelings is to engage in what is called expressive writing, where you summarize your thoughts and feelings by writing them down in an essay. Another approach is to engage in positive self-talk aimed at managing your feelings of anxiety, such as expressing in written or spoken words your confidence that you can deal with the learning task. Overall, give yourself the opportunity to learn with a clear mind that is not overwhelmed with negative thoughts of worry.

So What Should I Do?

Exercising the anxiety habit can be tricky but here are a few tactics you might want to try:

1. Write a paragraph that summarizes your feelings.
2. Give yourself a brief pep talk in which you spell out some positive thoughts.
3. Take some deep breaths to calm your body.
4. Use some of the tactics for the belief habit (Successful Habit #3) to help you see yourself as a capable learner, who is up to the challenge of mastering the material.

If you are not able to manage your anxiety related to academics on your own, the next step is to seek the help of mental health professionals. For example, biofeedback training, under the supervision of mental health professionals, has been shown to be effective in helping people control their anxiety and focus their attention for academic success.

Overall, it is fine to start by acknowledging your negative thoughts but you will need to find ways to create a more positive mental environment for learning, as summarized in the box.

BOX 9 How to Apply the Anxiety Habit

Do this:	Not this:
Clear your mind of negative thoughts while you study.	Welcome your worries into your study time, with hopes they will push you to study harder.

Sources

Aritzeta, A., Soroa, G., Balluerka, N., Muela, A., Gorostiaga, A., & Aliri, J. (2017). Reducing anxiety and improving academic performance through a biofeedback relaxation training program. *Applied Psychophysiology and Biofeedback, 42*, 193–202.

Huang, X., & Mayer, R. E. (2016). Benefits of adding anxiety-reducing features to a computer-based multimedia lesson. *Computers in Human Behavior, 63*, 293–303.

Maloney, E.A., & Beilock, S. L. (2012). Math anxiety: Who has it, why it develops, and how to guard against it. *Trends in Cognitive Science, 16*(8), 404–406.

Suinn, R. M., & Winston, E. H. (2003). The mathematics anxiety rating scale, a brief version: Psychometric data. *Psychological Reports, 92*, 176–173.

Successful Habit #10

Keep Your Mind Focused

Dan's Day Dreamin'

Dan is in the library study hall sitting at a time-worn study table with his own classic green desk lamp shining light down for him. The study hall has a huge vaulted ceiling and the walls are punctuated with long, stained glass windows. Today's task is to read a 25-page chunk of his history book, which has been assigned for tomorrow's class. Looking around at the other students busy with their laptops and notebooks, he opens his book and begins to read, feeling very much like he fills the role of a successful student.

As he reads, he thinks about the other students who have put in their study hall time and gone on to successful lives. He imagines himself coming back to this very spot years from now, feeling the glow of a successful life. He wonders what the other students around him might be studying. He imagines where they will be going when they leave the library. He thinks about the party he is planning for this weekend. He thinks about the bike ride he went on earlier this morning. He thinks about a problem his sister is having in high school. He even thinks about how much he loves chocolate, and imagines himself buying a candy bar.

By the time he is ready to take a break from reading, his mind has wandered near and far, and he finds that he has gone through most of the pages in his reading assignment. All in all, this is turning out to be a perfect study experience, Dan thinks to himself.

Concentrating on the Task at Hand

Dan's approach to reading his book is to let his mind wander as he reads. He thinks it makes him relax and enjoy the reading experience. Perhaps this sounds like a reasonable idea to you. To help you think this through, please place a checkmark next to the statements that make sense to you.

☐ A. Letting your mind wander as you read helps you relax and absorb the material.

☐ B. Letting your mind wander as you read fills your head with ideas that make you a more creative reader.

☐ C. Zoning out as you read is just another form of distraction that keeps you from deeply processing the material on the page.

☐ D. Students who engage in less mind wandering as they read tend to learn more.

If you checked A or B, you are taking a "glass is half full approach" to mind wandering by trying to find some positive aspects. Although there may be some circumstances in which mind wandering is helpful, mind wandering while studying is not one of them (Feng, D'Mello, & Graesser, 2013; Smallwood & Schooler, 2015). Mind wandering may help on tasks like creative problem solving, but it has been shown to be harmful to reading comprehension, particularly when the material is difficult (Feng, D'Mello, & Graesser, 2013). Thus, I regret to have to tell you that people who checked A or B are endorsing the habits of unsuccessful students.

How do we know someone's mind is wandering? One way is to give them a text to read and interrupt them at various points to ask if their mind is wandering (Smallwood & Schooler, 2015). Overall, research shows that people who engage in lots of mind wandering while reading perform more poorly on reading comprehension tests (Feng, D'Mello, & Graesser, 2013; Smallword & Schooler, 2015). Thus, if you want to take an evidence-based approach to mind wandering and join the ranks of successful students, you should check C and D rather than A and B.

What exactly is mind wandering? Mind wandering occurs when your attention shifts away from the primary task (such as reading a text or listening to a lecture) to thoughts that are unrelated to the task. How does mind wandering do its damage? Your cognitive capacity is limited, so you can only process a limited amount of information at any one time. In short, when you let your mind wander, you are creating a situation in which you must share your limited capacity with extraneous processing—that is, processing that is not relevant to your studying goal. When you use some of your limited cognitive capacity on extraneous processing, you have less capacity left to comprehend the material on the page. Your eyes may be looking at each word on the page, but you may not have the remaining cognitive capacity needed to make sense of the material. This is why mind wandering is particularly harmful when the material is difficult for you.

Mindfulness Habit

As you can see, when you let your mind wander while you are reading, studying, or attending class, you are displaying the habits of an unsuccessful student. The example of Dan's daydreaming suggests what can be called the *mindfulness habit: People learn better when they focus their attention on the task at hand.* In your quest to become a successful student, your goal should be to develop a habit of *mindfulness*—maintaining a state of focused attention for the task at hand.

So What Should I Do?

How do you develop a habit of mindfulness? Just telling yourself, "Pay attention, doofus!" is not an effective strategy for increasing your mindfulness. You need to learn to clear your head so you can focus your attention on the present task. This is not a matter of suppression of unwanted thoughts but rather a matter of openness to the present task. For your mindfulness training, you could try a form of meditation in which you practice each day for ten minutes on sitting in an upright posture with your eyes closed or your gaze lowered, focusing your attention on your breathing, trying to release distracting thoughts without elaborating on them, and letting your mind come to rest rather than actively suppressing unwanted thoughts. Research has shown this kind of mindfulness training can reduce mind wandering during reading and improve reading comprehension (Mrazek, Franklin, Phillips, Baird, & Schooler, 2013). Based on this work, I can recommend that you engage in a few minutes of daily practice on keeping your attention focused on your sensory experience, such as your breathing. You may need some expert training and guidance on how to practice for mindfulness. Learning to keep your mind open and ready for learning could help you become a successful student, as summarized in the box below.

BOX 10 How to Apply the Mindfulness Habit

Do this:	Not this:
Keep your attention focused on the learning task.	As you study, let your mind freely wander even if that means you are not thinking about the lesson.

Sources

Feng, S., D'Mello, S., & Graesser, A. C. (2013). Mind wandering while reading easy and difficult texts. *Psychonomic Bulletin and Review, 20,* 586–592.

Mrazek, M. D., Franklin, F. S., Phillips, D. T., Baird, B., & Schooler, J. (2013). Mindfulness training improves working memory capacity and GRE performance while reducing mind wandering. *Psychological Science, 24*(5), 776–781.

Smallwood, J., & Schooler, J. W. (2015). The science of mind wandering: Empirically navigating the stream of consciousness. *Annual Review of Psychology, 66,* 487–518.

Part 3
Means to Learn

Successful Habit #11

Reread Material that Needs Clarification

The Strange Case of Hermann Ebbinghaus

Suppose I ask you to read aloud the following list of nonsense syllables to yourself at the rate of one per second:

POS
MAF
REH
NIZ
VEQ
XAB
DUL
TOR

First you would say "P-O-S," wait a second and then say, "M-A-F," and so on. Then, I ask you to close the book, count aloud to 30, and write down as many of the triplets as you can, in order. If you are like most folks, you would not do very well on that learning task.

Suppose on another day, I give you an equivalent list of eight nonsense syllables, and ask you to read them aloud letter-by-letter at the rate of one triplet per second. Then, I ask you to do that again. Then, again and again and again one last time. Then, I ask you to close the book, count to 30, and write down as many of the triplets as you can in order. If you are like most folks, you did much better when you reread the list multiple times than when you read it just once.

In the late 1800s, Hermann Ebbinghaus conducted experiments like this, using himself as the only participant (Ebbinghaus, 1885/1964). He produced the first major principle of learning that is still principle #1 in the science of learning: The more times you go over material, the better you will remember it. Since this initial demonstration of the power of repetition, first published in 1885, the repetition effect has been replicated so many times that everyone has lost count.

What does the strange case of Hermann Ebbinghaus have to do with your academic success? A straightforward implication of the repetition effect for modern day learners seems to be: When you have a reading assignment, read the material and then reread it. Although this idea seems like common sense, let's explore whether rereading is an effective study strategy.

Does Rereading Work?

Does the repetition effect mean that you should read and then reread each assigned chapter in your textbook? Please place a checkmark next to each item that makes sense to you.

☐ A. Read and reread should be your #1 study strategy because it is the top choice of students.

☐ B. Read and reread should be your #1 study strategy because it comes from the #1 principle of learning.

☐ C. Read and reread may not be your best choice as a study strategy.

☐ D. Once you have read the material, rereading it is a waste of time.

Concerning option A, you are correct to agree with the idea that rereading is a popular study strategy. A recent review (Miyatsu, Nguyen, & McDaniel, 2018) found that of 1500 students who were surveyed across several different studies, 78 percent said they commonly used rereading as a study strategy. Part of the appeal of rereading may be that it is so easy to do. However, even though you are correct to think rereading is popular, you are not correct to conclude that it is always effective. Research shows that it often is not (Dunlosky, Rawson, Marsh, Nathan, & Willingham, 2013; Miyatsu, Nguyen, & McDaniel, 2018).

Concerning option B, you are correct to show respect for the power of study time as reflected in the repetition effect, but you are not correct to conclude that rereading is an effective way to use your study time. You should look at the repetition effect as telling you that the more time that you spend in focused study, the more you will learn (as was explored in Successful Habit #5 on the time habit). When you read and then immediately reread, the second reading may not be very helpful if you go through the motions of simply reading each word. More study time is helpful in improving your learning to the extent that you use it wisely. There may be other study strategies that are more effective ways to spend your study time, so option C deserves your checkmark.

Does this mean that rereading is completely useless as a study strategy? Actually, research shows that there are some ways to use rereading to improve your learning (Miyatsu, Nguyen, & McDaniel, 2018; Ponce & Mayer, 2014), so you might not want to be so fast to check option D. First, rereading is most effective when there is a suitable interval between the first and second reading (consistent with the spacing habit in Successful Habit #6) rather than when you read and then immediately reread. Second, rereading a short portion of your text may be appropriate when you detect a problem in your comprehension of the material. For example, as you read along you may realize that something you just read is not clear to you or that it seems to conflict with earlier material. Noticing how well you understand what you are reading is called *comprehension monitoring*. When you realize you are not understanding what you are reading or there appear to be conflicting statements, a useful remedy is to carefully reread the relevant parts of the text to help resolve the problem. This leads to deeper learning, which is the characteristic of successful studying. Third, rereading of relevant portions of the text can be useful when used in conjunction with other study strategies such as summarizing or outlining. In order to figure out what to put in your summary or outline, you may need to go back and reread relevant parts of the text.

Rereading Habit

The *rereading habit* is: *People learn better when they reread parts of the text that need clarification or that help support other study strategies such as summarizing or outlining.* In this case you are rereading a part of the text that is important for your understanding, perhaps so you can clarify it, summarize it, or outline it. The flip side of this habit is that rereading is not the most effective way to use your study time when you simply reread every word in a passage that you have just read.

Overall, the potential benefits of rereading depend on your purpose. If your approach is to reread parts of the text that need clarification or are needed to support another study strategy, this is an example of *strategic rereading* and is likely to improve your learning. If your approach is simply to reread every word without trying to make sense of the material, this is an example of *mechanical rereading* and is probably not the most effective way to improve your learning. To the extent that you engage in mechanical rereading, you are on the path to becoming an unsuccessful student. To avoid this fate and instead become a successful student, you will need to learn to use rereading strategically—to help you clarify confusing text or better use other study strategies such as summarizing or outlining.

So What Should I Do?

Rereading is a common study strategy that can be used effectively (i.e., to help you understand the material) or ineffectively (i.e., to help you repeat the material word-for-word without trying to understand it). To maximize your chances of using rereading effectively, I recommend that you try tactics like these:

1. As you are reading your textbook, stop when you realize you did not understand the sentence you just read and read it again to make sure you understand.
2. If necessary, also reread related sentences to help you resolve any discrepancies.
3. Locate parts of the text that are particularly important and reread them. Once you have reread, consider using related learning habits such as self-explaining (Successful Habit #19) or summarizing (Successful Habit 14).

The goal of rereading is not to help you remember the author's exact wording, but rather to help you understand the author's meaning, as summarized in the box below.

BOX 11 How to Apply the Rereading Habit	
Do this:	**Not this:**
When you come across a sentence in your textbook that confuses you or is important to understand, read it (and related material) again.	Read every word in a textbook section, and then read them all again.

Sources

Dunlosky, J., Rawson, K. A., Marsh, E. J., Nathan, M. J., & Willingham, D. T. (2013). Improving students' learning with effective learning techniques: Promising directions from cognitive and educational psychology. *Psychological Science in the Public Interest, 14*(1), 4–58.

Ebbinghaus, H. (1885/1964). *Memory.* New York: Dover. [Originally published in German in 1885.]

Miyatsu, T., Nguyen, K., & McDaniel, M. A. (2018). Five popular study strategies: Their pitfalls and optimal implementations. *Perspectives on Psychological Science, 13,* 390–407.

Ponce, H. R., & Mayer, R. E. (2014). Qualitatively different cognitive processing during online reading primed by different study activities. *Computers in Human Behavior, 30,* 121–130.

Successful Habit #12

Highlight Main Ideas as a First Step

Meet Markie the Marker

Marcus has a very tight relationship with his yellow markers. He loves the way the cap pops off and fits on the bottom, he loves the way the marker feels in his hand as he highlights text, and he even loves the way the ink smells as it spreads across the page. From the very first day of college, he got himself a huge collection of yellow highlighter pens which he stashes everywhere.

His friends teasingly call him "Markie the Marker" (or simply "Markie") because he always has a bright yellow marker in his pocket and he is not afraid to use it. He uses it when he reads his textbooks, highlighting what he sees as the main points on each page. He uses it to highlight what he likes when he reads over transcripts of the instructor's lectures, which he prints out from the course website. He uses it to highlight portions of email threads from the course blog that he prints out and keeps in his course binder. In short, if there is printed text on paper, Markie the Marker will not quit until all of his favorite phrases are highlighted in bright yellow.

Marcus is reading the introductory chapter in his philosophy textbook. He finds some fairly heavy ideas so he whips out his yellow marker. Page after page becomes full of yellow highlighting. Marcus sits back with a smile on his face as he blows on the tip of the marker, like he is blowing away the smoke from a newly fired pistol. He loves that his markers make him feel in charge of his own learning.

Really?

As you can see, Marcus—alias Markie the Marker— believes that highlighting is an effective study strategy. Really? What do you think? Please check each item you agree with:

☐ A. Highlighting turns the passive task of reading into an active task that improves learning.

☐ B. Highlighting must be effective because it is used by so many students.

☐ C. Highlighting often is ineffective.

☐ D. Highlighting is useless.

Option A has some appeal because it certainly is true that highlighting makes you behaviorally active, but research shows that it is cognitive activity that causes you to learn, not behavioral activity (Ponce & Mayer, 2014). There is no guarantee that every kind of hands-on activity will automatically translate into the cognitive processes needed for deep learning—attending to the relevant information, mentally organizing it into a coherent structure, and integrating it with relevant prior knowledge activated from long-term memory. Thus, you should not be lured into picking option A just because highlighting involves hands-on activity.

Option B also has some appeal because researchers have documented that highlighting is commonly used by students. In fact, a recent review (Miyatsu, Nguyen, & McDaniel, 2018) concluded that more than half of the students surveyed reported using highlighting as a study strategy while reading. However, just because something is popular does not mean that it is effective. In fact, research also shows (Dunlosky, Rawson, Marsh, Nathan, & Willingham, 2013; Miyatsu, Nguyen, & McDaniel, 2018) that highlighting often is ineffective, so you should not be lured into picking option B just because highlighting is popular.

As noted above, highlighting is a popular study strategy, but not necessarily an effective one, so option C deserves your checkmark. Some common problems are that students are too inexperienced to be able to distinguish between what is important and what is not, or their approach is to highlight nearly everything. Younger learners, in particular, tend to misuse highlighting (Miyatsu, Nguyen, McDaniel, 2018). In short, highlighting is not effective when students lack the needed metacognitive skills of being aware of what is important in a lesson.

Does this mean that highlighting is useless as stated in option D? Actually, research shows that there are conditions under which highlighting has been effective:

1. When students are experienced in how to use highlighting (such as for higher-performing or older students).
2. When students receive training and guidance in how to use highlighting.
3. When students use highlighting in conjunction with other study strategies, such as a prelude to writing a summary or an outline (Miyatsu, Nguyen, & McDaniel, 2018; Ponce & Mayer, 2014).

Thus, option D does not deserve your checkmark, so you may want to hold onto your yellow markers, maybe just as a backup. As you can see, becoming a successful student includes knowing how to use highlighting as a first step in deep learning.

Highlighting Habit

The learning strategy of highlighting includes underlining or marking important parts of a printed text. The *highlighting habit* is: *People do not necessarily learn better when they highlight as they read, but they can learn better when they know how to correctly highlight the main ideas in a printed text and follow-up with deeper study strategies (such as summarizing or outlining).*

The beauty of highlighting is that it is easy to use, but its pitfall is that it is easy to misuse (such as by highlighting too much or by highlighting unimportant material). On its own, as a self-taught strategy, highlighting may not quite give you the results you want even though it is easy to use and popular among your peers. You may need training and guidance in how to determine what is important in a lesson, such as learning how to form an outline showing the structure of the material. Once you can generate an outline, this will tell you what is important enough to be highlighted, and you may even want to number the elements you have highlighted and write in a heading indicating how they would fit into your outline. In other words, highlighting may be most effective when you know how to identify what is important and when you know how to use highlighting in conjunction with other study strategies such as summarizing (see Successful Habit #14) or outlining (see Successful Habit #15). In your quest to be a successful student, you will need to be careful in how you use that yellow marker of yours.

So What Should I Do?

Highlighting is a common study strategy that can be used effectively (i.e., to help you understand the material) or ineffectively (i.e., to help you memorize the printed material word-for-word). If you want to highlight for successful studying, I recommend that you consider the following tactics:

1. Get yourself a highlighting instrument you like (and some extras). Personally, I prefer to use a yellow highlighter (in fact, I always have one with me) but, of course, you should feel free to use a different colored highlighter, or to underline or circle with a pencil or pen.

2. When you find an important term that needs a definition, use your yellow highlighter to highlight it and also highlight a phrase that contains the definition. Perhaps use your pen to add an arrow from the term to the definition.

3. When you come across superordinate terms and subordinate terms (such as types of memory stores), use your yellow highlighter to highlight the subordinate terms (e.g., "sensory memory", "working memory", and "long-term memory") and the superordinate term (e.g., "memory stores"). Perhaps also use your pen to underline the superordinate term that is highlighted in yellow and add small numbers before each subordinate term that is highlighted in yellow (e.g., "1)", "2)", "3)"). Instead of highlighting the superordinate term, you could write on the page yourself, using your pen.

4. When you come across steps in a process, use your yellow highlighter to highlight the key phrase for each step, and then perhaps use your pen to add arrows or small numbers before each step. Also, highlight the name of the process and underline it, or simply write the name of the process next to the steps using your pen.

5. When you come to an important fact that you think you need to remember, use your yellow highlighter to highlight the main words (but not extra words that emphasize minor details). Perhaps use a pen to underline the most important information, such as a number or technical term.

6. Use highlighting in conjunction with other study strategies such as summarizing or mapping. For example, after you highlight a section of your textbook, you can then use your highlighted material to write a summary (based on the summarizing habit in Successful Habit #14) or write an outline (based on the mapping habit in Successful Habit #15).

Your goal in highlighting is to search for key terms and definitions, elements in a hierarchy (e.g., parts of a system), steps in a process, important facts, and any other chunks of information that are central to the lesson. If you just underline or mark every sentence that strikes your fancy, you will be losing out on the power of highlighting as a study aid.

BOX 12 How to Apply the Highlighting Habit

Do this:	Not this:
When you come across an important word or phrase, highlight it.	Highlight almost every sentence, so you can remember it.

Sources

Dunlosky, J., Rawson, K. A., Marsh, E. J., Nathan, M. J., & Willingham, D. T. (2013). Improving students' learning with effective learning techniques: Promising directions from cognitive and educational psychology. *Psychological Science in the Public Interest, 14*(1), 4–58.

Miyatsu, T., Nguyen, K., & McDaniel, M. A. (2018). Five popular study strategies: Their pitfalls and optimal implementations. *Perspectives on Psychological Science, 13,* 390–407.

Ponce, H., & Mayer, R. E. (2014). An eye-movement analysis of highlighting and graphic organizer study aids for learning from expository text. *Computers in Human Behavior, 41* 21–32.

Successful Habit #13

Use Flashcards for Limited Situations

Lucy's Lists and Francine's Flashcards

Lucy sees herself as a highly conscientious student. In her political science course, she notices that there are many unfamiliar terms used by her instructor and in her textbook. To study for an upcoming weekly quiz, she has gone through her textbook chapter and class notes for the first week, copying each term and its definition word-for-word on a yellow sheet. She figures that the act of copying over the definitions will reinforce them in her mind. This is a tedious process but Lucy is sure it will pay off when she takes the weekly quiz.

Her classmate, Francine, is never far from her pile of flashcards—3-by-5 index cards that have a term printed on one side and the definition on the other. Francine has carefully constructed them by going through her textbook and class notes for a class she is taking on political science. Each time she finds a new term she carefully prints it on one side of an index card, and prints the author or instructor's definition of the term on the other side. Just from the first chapter and the first week of lectures, she already has a hefty pile of flashcards held together by a thick rubber band. She whips out her flashcards whenever she has a few spare moments, such as riding the bus on the way to class, sitting on a bench between classes, or even in the cafeteria as she eats her lunch. Her procedure is always the same: She takes the top card and reads the term, she tries to think of the definition, she turns the card over and reads the definition to herself to see if she is right, and then she places the card on the bottom of the stack. In this way she tries to go through the deck many times during the course of the week.

Learning by Listing vs. Learning by Flipping

We could say that Lucy is studying by listing while Francine is studying by flipping. Is either one of them really using an effective study strategy? Even worse, is someone showing unsuccessful habits? Let's see what you think. Please place a check mark next to each statement you endorse:

☐ A. Copying down definitions word-for-word is probably not the best way to learn definitions.

☐ B. Using flashcards is preferable because this is what so many students do.

☐ C. Quizzing yourself with flashcards may not be the best way to learn most material, but it might be useful in some situations such as learning definitions of key terms.

☐ D. Both approaches are more effective than not going over your notes and textbook at all.

Maybe you think that copying down definitions is a useful strategy because it makes you actively interact with the material that you have read in the book or heard in the lecture. If so, you probably object to option A. However, when I look at Lucy, I am reminded of the wise adage: Hands-on activity does not cause learning, cognitive activity causes learning. Copying (i.e., writing down text word-for-word) or shadowing (i.e., repeating the words aloud) have been shown to be fairly ineffective ways to learn, even if they do involve hands-on activity (Dunlosky, Rawson, Marsh, Nathan, & Willingham, 2013; Miyatsu, Nguyen, & McDaniel, 2018). In contrast, summarizing the material in your words is effective (as discussed in Successful Habit #14 on the summarizing habit). If you opt for verbatim copying as your primary form of studying, you may be on the road to becoming an unsuccessful student. This is why I would check option A.

What about flashcards? If you checked option B, you are right about your assessment that flashcards are popular. A recent review (Miyatsu, Nguyen, & McDaniel, 2018) found that 55 percent of college students reported using flashcards to help them study at least sometimes. However, the research evidence does not support the use of flashcards as your primary study strategy (Dun-losky, Rawson, Marsh, Nathan, & Willingham, 2013; Miyatsu, Nguyen, & McDaniel, 2018), so I would be hesitant about checking option B. Like Francine, you can increase the effectiveness of flashcards if you go over them often (consistent with the time habit in Successful Habit #5) and you space out your practice over time (consistent with the spacing habit in Successful Habit #6). There also is some evidence that dropping well-learned flashcards can increase your efficiency but many students do not know how to drop flashcards—sometimes dropping them after only one correct trial (Kornell & Bjork, 2008).

When are flashcards useful? I must confess that flashcards are troubling to me because they seem to be used mainly to memorize isolated factoids rather than to foster deep understanding. However, I also must acknowledge that sometimes rote memorization is required, and in those few cases it might be appropriate to use flashcards. For example, flashcards have been shown to be effective in helping students remember definitions, medical terms, and foreign language vocabulary (Miyatsu, Nguyen, & McDaniel, 2018; Schmidmaier, Ebersbach, Schiller, Hege, Holzer, & Fischer, 2011). Thus, Francine is on the right track in using flashcards to learn definitions of key terms, and option C deserves a check mark. However, when using flashcards becomes your dominant approach to studying new concepts you may be acting like an unsuccessful student.

Finally, maybe you checked option D because you think doing something is better than doing nothing. I guess I have to agree as long as that something increases the time you spend thinking about the material (consistent with the time habit in Successful Habit #5). Unfortunately, mechanically copying material word-for-word probably does not cause you to think much about the material, thereby minimizing its usefulness as a study strategy. There are better ways to spend your study time for the bulk of your to-be-studied material if you want to be a successful student. In certain very limited circumstances (e.g., to memorize a few key definitions), you might consider using flashcards but this should be used in concert with other principles described in this section.

Pretraining Habit

I'll admit it, memorizing isolated pieces of information is not my favorite kind of studying. Thus, most of this book is devoted to helping you understand the material rather than simply remembering it. However, I also have to admit that sometimes in a course there may be a small amount of material that does need to be memorized. For example, in a math course you may need to memorize the definitions of key terms or the formulas for key computations; in a physiology course, you may need to memorize the names and locations of each of the bones in the human body; in a computer programming course, you may need to memorize the names and definitions of the main commands; and in a foreign language course you may need to memorize the vocabulary words such as "dog" in English means "perro" in Spanish. In these cases, memorizing the basic facts can help you to be able to devote your attention to understanding the conceptual material in a lesson.

This leads to the *pretraining habit: People learn challenging conceptual material better when they already know the names and characteristics of the key terms.* Brute force methods such as copying or repeating pieces of text, word-for-word, are particularly unappealing and ineffective, but other mnemonic techniques can be effective in memorizing isolated pieces of information. *Mnemonic techniques* are methods for rote memorizing. For example, when you want to memorize the answer to a question or the definition of a term, carefully constructed regimens of flashcards may be effective—especially when used in conjunction with spacing (as discussed in Successful Habit #6) and interleaving (as discussed in Successful Habit #7) and self-testing (as discussed in Successful Habit #17). Although using flashcards may be considered a limited form of self-testing, focusing on learning paired-associates such as definitions, research shows that giving yourself practice tests on the broader material can be an effective strategy. This broader form of self-testing is examined in Successful Habit #17.

The *keyword method* is perhaps the best-established mnemonic technique for memorizing paired-associates (such as translating a word from one language to another).

In the keyword method you start with the stimulus word—such as "perro" and turn it into a keyword that has a similar sound such as the nice green fruit "pear." This is the acoustic link. Then, you form a mental image of the response word, "dog," interacting with the keyword, such as a dog walking happily along with a pear in its mouth. This is the imagery link. Then, when I ask you what does "perro" mean, you can remember "pear" which reminds you of the dog walking along with a pear in its mouth, so you say "dog." The keyword method can be extremely effective in niche situations such as memorizing foreign language vocabulary, but students tend to stay away from the keyword method because it is so tedious to use. Students need extensive training and may need help in constructing keywords.

Overall, mnemonic techniques such as the keyword method or flashcards may be successfully used in situations where you have to memorize pairs—such as terms and definitions or foreign language vocabulary—but they can be hard to use and should consume only a small portion of your study time.

So What Should I Do?

Flashcards are a common tool used in studying, so let's look at some suggestions for how to use them most effectively for successful studying:

1. Get yourself a nice supply of 3 x 5-inch index cards (or another size if you prefer) and some rubber bands.

I prefer plain white index cards, but you may want to use lined cards and/or cards in light colors such as pink, yellow, blue, etc.

2. To learn definitions, select the key terms and definitions from your lesson. Write the term on one side and the definition on the other, using as few words as necessary.

3. To learn second language vocabulary, write the word in one language on one side and the word in the other language on the other side. For example, you could have "perro" on one side and "dog" on the other, if you want to practice translating from Spanish to English.

4. Develop a plan for how to manage your stack of cards. It is best to limit the deck to a manageable size for you, perhaps based on one chapter or one lecture. It is also more effective to drop a card once you have mastered it (e.g., after getting it right three times in a row). Once you have your stack ready to go, you can go through it over and over. Look at the top side containing the key term, for example, and try to recite the definition. Then, flip it over to see if you were right. If so, put a little check mark in the corner (or just fold the corner, or devise some other system for keeping track); if you were wrong, put a little X in the corner (or unfold a corner). When you are right three times in row, move the flashcard to the "mastered stack" and proudly put a rubber band around it. Keep working until all the cards are moved to the mastered pile.

5. Use the spacing habit (Successful Habit #6), interleaving habit (Successful Habit #7), and self-testing habit (Successful Habit #17) in conjunction with your flashcards. You will also have to manage your time based on the time habit (Successful Habit #5).

Flashcards are not my favorite study strategy but they can serve a niche function in helping you master some key terms. This can make it easier for you to go on to learn the main material with deeper understanding, and thus flashcards can help you become a successful student when you restrict their use to appropriate material.

BOX 13 How to Apply the Pretraining Habit	
Do this:	**Not this:**
Learn the meanings of the key terms before you focus on understanding the material.	Just learn the material without worrying about already knowing the key terms.

Sources

Dunlosky, J., Rawson, K. A., Marsh, E. J., Nathan, M. J., & Willingham, D. T. (2013). Improving students' learning with effective learning techniques: Promising directions from cognitive and educational psychology. *Psychological Science in the Public Interest, 14*(1), 4–58.

Kornell, N., & Bjork, R. A. (2008). Optimising self-regulated study: The benefits—and costs—of dropping flashcards. *Memory, 16,* 125–136.

Miyatsu, T., Nguyen, K., & McDaniel, M. A. (2018). Five popular study strategies: Their pitfalls and optimal implementations. *Perspectives on Psychological Science, 13,* 390–407.

Schmidmaier, R., Ebersbach, R., Schiller, M., Hege, I., Holzer, M., & Fischer, M. R. (2011). Using electronic flashcards to promote learning in medical students: Retesting versus restudying. *Medical Education, 45,* 1001–1110.

Successful Habit #14

Summarize in Your Own Words

Carrie the Copier

Carrie is sitting in the first row of her statistics class, waiting for class to begin, with her notebook wide open and her pencil clenched in her hand. As soon as the instructor starts talking, she perks up and tries to write down every word that he says. Sometimes she may miss a few, but she knows it is important to write down as many of his words as possible. The same goes for his writing on the board. Carrie tries to make sure that everything on the board gets copied into her notebook.

For example, when the instructor says, "Today we will be exploring the wonderful world of standard deviation, which reminds me of the time I took a trip to Colorado," she writes in her notebook, "Today-exploring wonderful world of standard deviation-reminds me of trip to Colorado."

Carrie prides herself in her excellent notetaking skills. The way she sees it, her notes should be a transcript of what the instructor said, so when she goes back to study them, she will have the lecture there in her notebook. What is better to study than the words from the instructor's mouth?

What's Wrong with Copying?

You might think that Carrie is an excellent student, who exhibits exemplary study skills. Although I must agree that she is a conscientious student, I think we should carefully consider whether she is an effective student. Please check the items that you endorse:

☐ A. Notetaking is not an effective study strategy because it distracts you from paying attention to the lecture or text.

☐ B. Notetaking is a popular study strategy so it must be effective.

☐ C. Verbatim notetaking is an excellent study strategy.

☐ D. Summary notetaking is an excellent study strategy.

If you are prone to check option A, you probably are asking yourself: "Why take notes at all?" You may think to yourself: "If I am busy writing words down (or typing on a laptop), I can't pay attention to or think about what is being said." On the surface, you appear to make some good points, but research shows that using active learning strategies such as notetaking during a lecture can greatly improve your learning if you implement them effectively

(Dunlosky, Rawson, Marsh, Nathan, & Willingham, 2013; Miyatsu, Nguyen, & McDaniel, 2018; Fiorella & Mayer, 2015). For this reason, you might want to hold up on checking option A.

Option B also looks appealing because it is true that note-taking is a popular study strategy. In a recent review of over 1500 students from several different published studies (Miyatsu, Nguyen, & McDaniel, 2018), 30 percent of the students reported regularly using notetaking to help them learn. However, not all forms of notetaking are effective, so you should refrain from checking option B. Just because you take notes does not necessarily mean your learning will improve. You need to figure out how to take effective notes, so let's continue with the next options.

You can see that Carrie the Copier is a proponent of option C, but Carrie's view of how learning works conflicts with what we now know about the science of learning. Let's consider how notetaking can affect cognitive processing during learning. For meaningful learning to occur you need to engage in three kinds of cognitive processing during learning (Fiorella & Mayer, 2015):

selecting—paying attention to the relevant material.
organizing—mentally arranging the incoming material into a coherent structure.
integrating—mentally connecting incoming information with your relevant prior knowledge activated from long-term memory.

When you take verbatim notes like Carrie you are using up your limited cognitive processing capacity by focusing on as many of the words as you can. This leaves no more cognitive capacity to figure out what is important (i.e., selecting) or to reorganize the material (i.e., organizing) or to relate it with what you already know (i.e., integrating). You may be able to memorize some strings of words but you are not engaging in cognitive processing that supports meaningful learning. Thus, Carrie's approach is not likely to lead to success on tests that require understanding of the material.

On the other hand, with option D, you are using notetaking in a way that can lead to meaningful learning. When you summarize, you have to think about what is important enough to put into your summary (i.e., selecting), you have to organize the selected material into the structure of a paragraph (i.e., organizing), and you have to put it in your words (i.e., integrating). Research shows that summarizing as you read or listen improves test performance an average of .5 standard deviations, which is enough to increase your grade by at least one level (Fiorella & Mayer, 2015).

Summarizing Habit

When you use the study strategy of summarizing, you are restating the main ideas in a lesson in your own words, usually by writing a summary. The *summarizing habit* is: *People learn better when they summarize the main ideas in a lesson in their own words.* In order to avoid using unsuccessful study habits like Carrie the Copier does, you can become a successful student by taking summary notes and getting some guidance from your instructor or more successful peers on how well you are doing.

As we have seen, notetaking is a common learning strategy, but it can be used in many ways. In a classroom, you may see Luke who sits at his computer and types in a transcript of what the instructor is saying, like a court recorder. Next to him is Luz, who sits at her computer and types in summary notes that are concise, organized, and in Luz's own words. Both are working hard to take notes, but Luke is using an unsuccessful study habit while Luz is using a successful one.

So What Should I Do?

Based on what we know about the summarizing habit, I recommend you consider trying one of the following ways to summarize:

1. When you are listening to a lecture, write summary notes in your notebook. Begin the page with today's date and lecture topic, and just write down the main ideas in your own words as a summary. Use as few words as needed to create a summary that makes sense to you. Do not try to write down everything the instructor says or everything that is on the slides.
2. When you are reading your textbook, write summary notes in your notebook, or in the margins of the book, following the same procedure as for taking notes in a lecture.

3. Use the summarizing habit in conjunction with other study strategies such as highlighting (Successful Habit #12) or outlining (Successful Habit #15).

The goal of summarizing is to help you select what is important and organize it into a coherent structure that you express in your own words. The essence of how to apply the summarizing habit is shown in the box below.

BOX 14 Applying the Summarizing Habit	
Do this:	**Not this:**
Summarize the main ideas in a lesson in your own words.	Write down what the instructor says and what is on the slides word-for-word.

Sources

Dunlosky, J., Rawson, K. A., Marsh, E. J., Nathan, M. J., & Willingham, D. T. (2013). Improving students' learning with effective learning techniques: Promising directions from cognitive and educational psychology. *Psychological Science in the Public Interest, 14*(1), 4–58.

Fiorella, L., & Mayer, R. E. (2015). *Learning as a generative activity: Eight learning strategies that promote understanding.* New York: Cambridge University Press.

Miyatsu, T., Nguyen, K., & McDaniel, M. A. (2018). Five popular study strategies: Their pitfalls and optimal implementations. *Perspectives on Psychological Science, 13,* 390–407.

Successful Habit #15

Create Knowledge Maps

Give It a Try

Let me ask you to go back to the introduction to this book, and look at the second section entitled "The Search for Academic Success." Use a pencil and no more than one sheet of paper to take notes as you read over the introduction. Go ahead and give yourself two or three minutes to try this.

If you are like most students, your notes look like a list of sentences or phrases such as exemplified in the following box.

> motive-opportunity-means (MOM)
> become a successful learner
> search for academic success
> establish motive for learning
> create conditions for academic learning
> array of effective learning strategies
> remember MOM when you want to learn

Do your notes look like the list of phrases in the box? If so, you are using a list strategy for taking notes.

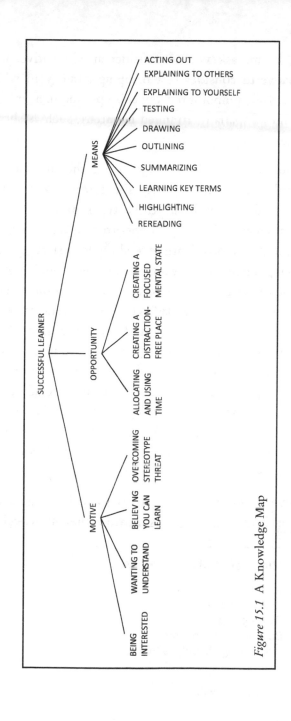

Figure 15.1 A Knowledge Map

Next, let me ask you to consider an alternative. One alternative to consider is a mapping strategy in which you carefully pinpoint the key concepts and then arrange them into a spatially arranged hierarchy, such as shown in Figure 15.1.

As you can see, the knowledge map in the box is a hierarchy that starts with "successful learner" at the top, which is linked with the three types or functions of study strategies—"motive," "opportunity," and "means." Then, under "motive" are several types of strategy such as "being interested," "wanting to understand," "believing you can learn," and "overcoming stereotype threat." Then, under "opportunity" you have several types of strategy such as "allocating and managing time," "creating a distraction-free place," and "creating a focused mental state." Finally, under "means" you have lines to several types of strategy ranging from "rereading" to "acting out." When a knowledge map takes the form of a hierarchy as in Figure 15.1, the key concepts are the nodes and they are connected by lines that denote relationships such as "type of" or "example of".

Another, more common way to spatially arrange this material is an outline, such as shown in the following box.

Functions of study strategies

Motive
 Being interested
 Wanting to understand
 Believing you can learn
 Overcoming stereotype threat

```
Opportunity
    Allocating and using time
    Creating a distraction-free place
    Creating a focused mental state
Means
    Rereading
    Highlighting
    Learning key terms
    Summarizing
    Outlining (...)
```

Outlining is a form of mapping because the key ideas are spatially arranged on the page or screen, with the subtopics indicated by indentation.

To List or To Map, That Is the Question

Which approach is most likely to lead to academic success? Please check the options you agree with:

☐ A. Notetaking by listing is best because it is easy to do and reminds you of the key information as it was presented in the lesson.

☐ B. Notetaking by mapping is tedious and confusing, so it should be avoided.

☐ C. Notetaking by mapping is best because it causes learners to select the important concepts and arrange them into a coherent spatial structure.

☐ D. Notetaking by listing causes learners to remember isolated factoids, which is sub-optimal.

You might look at the list in the first box and think to yourself, "What a nice job! The student has picked out some key information and put it into a neat list." If so, you probably checked option A.

Also, you might look at the knowledge map in the second box and think to yourself, "That takes a lot of work and is really complicated. This is just not how normal people take notes." The same reaction even applies to the outline in the third box. If this is your reaction to mapping, then you probably checked option B.

You would also be correct in assuming that a list strategy is commonly used in notetaking (Fiorella & Mayer, 2017; Miyatsu, Nguyen, & McDaniel, 2018), but when I look at students who take notes by generating a disconnected list of phrases, I am worried. Taking notes by writing a list of phrases may be a common strategy for students, but it is not the most effective strategy (Dunlosky, Rawson, Marsh, Nathan & Willingham, 2013). You would also be correct in assuming that it is not common to find students who spontaneously use mapping strategies (Fiorella & Mayer, 2017); however, my take is that they could be more successful students if they did. If you use a list writing strategy such as exemplified in the first box and you checked options A and B, you are well on your way to studying like an unsuccessful student.

At this point you might be asking, "So, if the list strategy is sub-optimal, what strategy should I be using?" Taking notes by mapping is one strategy that has been shown to be effective, especially when students receive training and support in how to create knowledge maps (Fiorella & Mayer, 2015; Miyatsu, Nguyen, & McDaniel, 2018; Ponce, Lopez, & Mayer, 2012). For this reason, I would opt for C and D. This is the approach of a successful student.

The rationale for mapping is that it causes you to engage in effective cognitive processing during learning such as selecting relevant material, mentally organizing it into a coherent structure, and integrating it with relevant prior knowledge. In short mapping supports the cognitive processes of:

> *selecting*—you must carefully choose the key concepts to use as nodes in your knowledge map.
> *organizing*—you must build a hierarchy (or outline) that shows the relations among the concepts.
> *integrating*—in thinking about how to translate from running text into a spatial arrangement you need to use your existing knowledge.

In contrast, in listing you are mainly copying key phrases without trying to see how everything fits together.

There are several kinds of mapping structures you can build, but the most common ones are:

> *hierarchy*—a superordinate concept is on top and it is linked by "example of" or "type of" lines with subordinate concepts, such as shown in the second box.
> *matrix*—a table with rows corresponding to two or more concepts and columns corresponding to

dimensions along which they are compared, such as comparing two breeds of dog on characteristics such as average weight, average lifespan, temperament, and common ailments.

flow chart—a series of boxes with arrows among them showing the steps in a process, such as the steps in how one neuron communicates with another.

outline—the most common form of mapping, which contains key concepts and subordinate concepts represented by the degree of indentation, as exemplified in the third box.

When you convert text into a hierarchy or a matrix or a flow chart or an outline, you have to engage in deep cognitive processing that helps you encode the material more meaningfully—making you a successful student.

The Mapping Habit

As you can see, in your quest to become a successful student, I urge you to consider the *mapping habit: People learn better when they create knowledge maps (including outlines) that spatially represent the content of the instructional text.* Don't get me wrong, mapping can be a tedious and confusing process. The remedy is to make sure you get guidance and support in how to construct knowledge maps, and that you practice enough to feel confident in your mapping expertise. Also, it makes sense to use mapping sparingly, and especially for material that neatly fits in a hierarchy, matrix, or flow chart.

A very basic form of mapping is outlining, which may be appropriate when you have a lot of text to read. In outlining, you are also using space to represent the organization of the text, by selecting the key ideas to be lined up against the left margin with subordinate ideas on indented lines under each one of them, and so on. Like any mapping strategy, outlining works because it prompts you to select key material, organize it into a coherent structure, and use your prior knowledge to translate from printed text to an outline.

Certainly taking any form of notes—even linear notes—is probably more effective than taking no notes, but research has shown that people who take notes by listing do not engage in as deep cognitive processing (indicated by their eye movements) as those who take notes by creating a knowledge map such as a matrix (Ponce & Mayer, 2014). Fortunately, learning to take notes by mapping (including outlining) is a learnable skill. If you can shift from taking notes by listing to taking notes by mapping, you are shifting from the habits of an unsuccessful student to the habits of a successful one. The power of mapping will help you achieve academic success.

So What Should I Do?

In order to use the mapping habit effectively, I suggest you consider trying one or more of the following tactics:

1. As you read your textbook, write an outline in your notebook (or in the margins of your book); or as you read over your lecture notes, write an outline

in nearby space in your notebook; or as you listen to a lecture, write an outline in your notebook. For each situation, start with today's date and the topic of the material. Try to capture the top-level headings in a few words and try to use parallel construction, writing each one on its own line along the left margin; under each top-level heading, try to write the second-level headings in a few words with each on its own line (but indent a few spaces), and so on. For example, the top two levels of the outline for the conclusion chapter in this book could be:

Motivational Habits
    Value
    Goal
    Belief
    Threat
Management Habits
    Time
    Spacing
    Interleaving
    Multitasking
    Anxiety
    Mindfulness
Learning Habits
    Rereading
    Highlighting
    Pretraining
    Summarizing

Mapping
Drawing
Self-testing
Self-explaining
Teaching
Enacting

You could go on and add a third level, such as the definition of each habit.

2. As you listen to a lecture or read your textbook or read over your lecture notes, create a knowledge map in your notebook, using an approach like that for outlining described previously. For example, for the conclusion chapter of the book, start by writing the top-level concepts across the top of the page, perhaps putting each in an oval or rectangle, and then under them write the second-level concepts perhaps putting each in an oval or rectangle and a connecting line back up to the top-level concept.

3. Use knowledge mapping for important chunks of information such as hierarchies, matrices, or flow charts.

4. Use outlining in conjunction with learning habits such as highlighting (see Successful Habit #12) and summarizing (see Successful Habit #14).

The key feature of mapping is that you are translating from linear text into a spatial arrangement of selected bits of the text. This helps you focus on what is important and how everything fits together.

The box below summarizes the do's and don'ts of applying the mapping habit.

Box 15: Applying the Mapping Habit	
Do this:	**Not this:**
Create an outline or knowledge map of the material in the lesson.	Create a list of the facts in the lesson.

Sources

Dunlosky, J., Rawson, K. A., Marsh, E. J., Nathan, M. J., & Willingham, D. T. (2013). Improving students' learning with effective learning techniques: Promising directions from cognitive and educational psychology. *Psychological Science in the Public Interest, 14*(1), 4–58.

Fiorella, L., & Mayer, R. E. (2015). *Learning as a generative activity: Eight learning strategies that promote understanding.* New York: Cambridge University Press.

Fiorella, L., & Mayer, R. E. (2017). Spontaneous spatial strategies in learning from scientific text. *Contemporary Educational Psychology, 49*, 66–79.

Miyatsu, T., Nguyen, K., & McDaniel, M. A. (2018). Five popular study strategies: Their pitfalls and optimal implementations. *Perspectives on Psychological Science, 13*, 390–407.

Ponce, H. R., Lopez, M. J., & Mayer, R. E. (2012). Instructional effectiveness of a computer-supported program for teaching reading comprehension strategies. *Computers & Education, 59*, 1170–1183.

Ponce, H. R., & Mayer, R. E. (2014). Qualitatively different cognitive processing during online reading primed by different study activities. *Computers in Human Behavior, 30*, 121–130.

Successful Habit #16

Make Drawings

How Fran Stays Focused

Fran is excited about her neuroscience course, and although the course is just beginning this week, she is eager to start reading her textbook. She glides over to her favorite spot in the library, sits down, and delicately places her open book on the table. Her assigned reading starts with a section on the process of neural transmission, which explains how one nerve cell communicates with another. It begins with a description of the structure of nerve cells and contains lots of technical terms like "neuron," "cell body," "axon," and "dendrite," just to name a few. Fran wants to stay super-focused on the book, so she makes sure there is no pencil and paper to distract her. She silently reads every word in every sentence, trying not to think of anything else but the words in that book.

In another part of the library, Frank also is reading about neural transmission in his neuroscience textbook. His approach to studying is a little different than Fran's. He

119

has opened his notebook to a blank page and he is holding his newly sharpened pencil in his hand. After reading a paragraph that describes the structure of a neuron, he tries to sketch out a drawing that contains each of the main parts described in the text, with a label for each one. He does the same for the next section that describes communication between neurons across a synapse, and so on. Eventually, he comes away with a collection of drawings that depict the material described in the textbook. He is not a particularly good artist so he does not try to create an artistically perfect rendering, but rather just a crude layout of the main parts in the system and the steps in the process.

Let's Be Frank about Fran

As you look at how these two students go about the task of studying their textbook, what is your assessment? Check the statements that you agree with.

☐ A. Fran is a dedicated and effective student, who knows how to focus her attention on the textbook.

☐ B. Frank is distracting himself by trying to draw rather than focusing on what the textbook author has to say.

☐ C. Fran does not appear to be trying to make sense of the material.

☐ D. By translating from words to drawings, Frank is trying to make sense of the material.

You might say to yourself, "Fran is really a dedicated student. She focuses her attention on the textbook." If so, you probably checked option A. However, when I look at what Fran is doing, I get worried that she may be so focused on memorizing the author's words that she is not actually understanding the main ideas. Accordingly, I would check C. Although Fran may be dedicated, she is showing the characteristics of an unsuccessful student by not trying to make sense of the material. If she wants to be successful, her job is not just to read every word in the textbook; it also is to understand what the author is saying.

You might look at Frank and wonder why he is distracting himself with making drawings, when he should be focusing on what the textbook author has to say. If so you probably checked option B. However, when I look at what Frank is doing, I see someone who is trying to make sense of the material—the hallmark of a successful student. In translating from words to drawings, Frank has to focus on the key terms, figure out how they relate to one another, and even relate the material to his prior knowledge. In short, I see that Frank is trying to engage in sense-making, which is what successful students do. If you agree with my assessment, you would check D.

The Drawing Habit

Don't get me wrong. Fran is off to a good start by reading her textbook chapter, but she is exhibiting the study habits of an unsuccessful student if that is all she does.

In order to become a sense-maker, she needs to apply a learning strategy that will encourage her to process the text more deeply. Frank is using just such a learning strategy—drawing, in which he creates an illustration that depicts the key material that is described in the text. Learning by drawing has been shown to be an effective learning strategy, especially when students read scientific text (Dunlosky, Rawson, Marsh, Nathan & Willingham, 2013; Fiorella & Mayer, 2015; Leutner & Schmeck, 2014; Schmeck, Mayer, Opfermann, Pfeiffer, & Leutner, 2014). Drawing can be most effective when it accomplishes these three cognitive goals:

1. selecting—when you have to pick elements to put in your drawing, you are encouraged to focus on the important parts of the text.
2. organizing—when you have to put the parts together into a drawing, this helps you arrange the key elements into a coherent structure.
3. integrating—when you have to translate from words to pictures, this causes you to use your relevant prior knowledge from long-term memory (Fiorella & Mayer, 2015).

For these reasons, I can recommend that you consider the *drawing habit* when you are studying text material: *People learn better when they create drawings that depict the content of instructional text.* The drawing habit works best when you have some support during learning, such as knowing which elements to include in your drawing (Fiorella & Mayer, 2015; Leutner & Schmeck, 2014). Another form of support is to minimize the effort needed for the mechanics of drawing, by being able to copy or create simple schematic components rather than having to draw an artistically beautiful and realistic illustration from scratch. The drawing habit also works best when you have had some training and practice in creating drawings for instructional text, so this is a learning strategy that is likely to become more helpful as you gain more experience with it (Fiorella & Mayer, 2015; Leutner & Schmeck, 2014).

Drawing is a learning strategy that takes a bit of effort on the part of learner, but it has been shown to be effective at least for short sections of science text. You might want to try it for those few sections of your textbook that describe how a system works—such as the process of neural transmission—rather than for sections that simply state facts or tell stories. Even if your textbook already has an illustration depicting how a cause-and-effect system works, it is worth your while to create your own drawing before looking at the one in the book. In this way, you can use the drawing habit sparingly, applying it mainly to help you understand any cause-and-effect systems that are presented in your textbook. If you can draw a coherent illustration, you are well on your way to becoming a successful student.

A somewhat related study strategy is based on the *imagining habit: People learn better when they form mental images that illustrate the text content in a lesson.* In the example at the start of this chapter, instead of drawing a diagram to represent neural transmission, Frank could simply imagine what the diagram would look like. Learning by imagining works when the learner selects the appropriate elements to be included in the image, mentally arranges them into a coherent spatial structure, and uses relevant prior knowledge in the process of translating from words to images. Learning by imagining has been shown to improve test performance, and may be most effective when you have sufficient prior knowledge and training, and when you are given guidance in what to include in the image (Fiorella & Mayer, 2015; Leopold & Mayer, 2015). You can try out learning by imagining to see if you can get it to work for you, especially when you are reading an imagery-friendly text that explains how a system works. Learning by drawing and learning by imagining are learning strategies that allow you to avoid the unsuccessful habit of reading without thinking.

So What Should I Do?

The drawing habit can be tricky to implement so let me offer a few suggestions:

1. Start with a nice sharp pencil and a concise list of the parts you want to include in your diagram. Your drawing should include only the parts in your list.
2. Keep your drawing simple (or schematic) with no extra details and no need for realism or artistic perfection.
3. Label the parts and add arrows or annotation as needed.

This is not a work of art to share with the world, but rather a form of notetaking for your personal use. The act of creating the illustration can be helpful in your quest to become a successful student, even if you don't feel like much of an artist. Box 16 gives you the do's and don'ts of applying the drawing habit.

Box 16 Applying the Drawing Habit

Do this:	Not this:
Create a drawing that depicts the main process or structure described in the text, and label each part.	Read each sentence in your textbook without using a pencil to distract you.

Sources

Dunlosky, J., Rawson, K. A., Marsh, E. J., Nathan, M. J., & Willingham, D. T. (2013). Improving students' learning with effective learning techniques: Promising directions from cognitive and educational psychology. *Psychological Science in the Public Interest, 14*(1), 4–58.

Fiorella, L., & Mayer, R. E. (2015). *Learning as a generative activity: Eight learning strategies that promote understanding.* New York: Cambridge University Press.

Leopold, C., & Mayer, R. E. (2015). An imagination effect in learning from scientific text. *Journal of Educational Psychology, 107*, 47–63.

Leutner, D., & Schmeck, A. (2014). The drawing principle in multimedia learning. In R. E. Mayer (Ed.), *The Cambridge handbook of multimedia learning* (2nd cd; pp. 433–448). New York: Cambridge University Press.

Schmeck, A., Mayer, R. E., Opfermann, M., Pfeiffer, V., & Leutner, D. (2014). Drawing pictures during learning from scientific text: Testing the generative drawing effect and the prognostic drawing effect. *Contemporary Educational Psychology, 39*, 275–286.

Successful Habit #17

Give Yourself Practice Tests

When Roommates Disagree

Jen and Jan are dorm roommates and they tend to do everything together. They wake up at the same time, they eat their meals together in the cafeteria, and they even happen to be taking the same psychology course this term. Both consider themselves to be conscientious students. They go to every lecture, they take notes on the lecture, they read the book as assigned, and they take notes on the book. So far, you can see they are in perfect agreement.

They each set aside the same amount of study time throughout the week but they use that time a little differently. Jen uses the time to review videos of the lectures available on the course website, read over her lecture notes, read over the chapter again, and read over her book notes. She calls this her "power-study mode" because she is concentrating her study time on studying the material. Jen thinks to herself, "What could be better than this?"

In contrast, Jan briefly looks over her notes just to refresh her memory. Then, she sits at her desk with her laptop computer and types in answers to test questions covering the material in the lecture and the book. She has collected questions from past exams that the instructor provided on the course website. Although the instructor says she will not necessarily use these specific questions on the exam, she will use questions like them. For example, one of the questions from this week's material on the social bases of behavior is: "Explain what stereotype threat is." Jan knows that she would have about five minutes to answer each question on the exam, so she gives herself five minutes to answer each of her practice questions. Jan thinks to herself, "What could be better than this?"

What Do You Think?

Who do you think is being a more effective student? Check each item that you agree with:

- ☐ A. Jen, because she is engaged in heavy-duty studying of the actual course material, making sure she knows what the instructor said and what the book said.

- ☐ B. Not Jan, because Jan is spending her time making up answers that may be wrong rather than focusing on studying the presented material.

- ☐ C. Jan, because she is engaged in deeper processing by giving herself practice in retrieving and using the material from her memory—just as she will have to do on the exam.

☐ D. Not Jen, because reviewing the same material over and over and over is boring and will lead to memorizing factoids rather than understanding the material.

The case for Jen might seem airtight: If the goal is to learn the material, the best approach is to study it and restudy it and restudy it again. This line of thinking would cause you to check A and B.

On the surface, this might sound like a good idea but let's consider Jen and Jan's immediate goal, which is to perform well on answering essay questions about the material. Does Jen's approach prepare her for this goal? Well, getting the material into her long-term memory is certainly a good start, and actually is indispensable to her success. Thus, some amount of reviewing of the material is needed. However, that is just half of the story. For the exam, she also needs to be able to retrieve the material from her long-term memory and use it to answer questions. The best way to accomplish that second goal is to practice on the target task—in this case, on answering exam-like questions as Jan is doing. Research shows that students perform better on a delayed test when they engage in reviewing and self-testing rather than on reviewing and more reviewing (Brown, Roediger, & McDaniel, 2014; Dunlosky, Rawson, Marsh, Nathan, & Willingham, 2013; Fiorella & Mayer, 2015). For these reasons, you should check C and D to show you favor successful learning habits.

How does self-testing work? A fundamental principle in the science of learning is that performance improves on a complex cognitive task (such as answering a test question) when you have: (a) the needed background knowledge, and (b) practice on the task. In short, you need both the knowledge (which you may strengthen through reviewing) and the ability to use that knowledge on the target task (which you may strengthen through self-testing). By practicing on retrieving information from your memory and organizing it in line with the requirements of the question, you are exercising the same skill that you will need on the exam. Of course, self-testing works best if you are able to detect and correct any difficulties you had in answering the question.

Self-Testing Habit

The story of Jen and Jan demonstrates the value of adding a new learning strategy to your toolbox—*self-testing*. *Self-testing involves giving yourself practice tests that are similar to the test you will have to take for the course.* This allows me to propose the *self-testing habit*: People learn better when they review and take practice tests than when they review and review again. As you can see, the learning strategy of self-testing belongs in the toolbox of anyone who wants to become a successful student. Overall, my recommendation is clear: Instead of spending all of your study time reviewing the presented material (such as rereading your notes, reviewing a video of the lecture, or rereading a book chapter), spend part of your time reviewing and part of your time taking practice tests.

So What Should I Do?

Self-testing can be a daunting task, so let me make a few suggestions:

1. Allocate a portion (even a small portion) of your study time to self-testing, to be used after you review the material and employ some of the other learning habits. You can exercise the self-testing habit orally, in writing, or by typing.
2. For each section of a book chapter or lecture, try to write down (or simply say) all you can remember. This is the classic version of self-testing because it focuses on recalling the material. In contrast, tactics 3 and 4 go a bit beyond traditional research on self-testing.
3. Decide on a question format that corresponds to that used on the exam. If the exam will contain essay questions, practice on writing essay answers. If the exam contains computational problems to be solved, practice on solving computational problems. If the exam consists of multiple choice items focused on specific facts, practice on these kinds of items.
4. If possible and if you have time, rate your confidence on a scale from 1 (very unconfident) to 10 (very confident) for each answer, and then compare your answer to the right answer (based on your textbook or lecture notes). Go back to your book and notes to review any material you had trouble with.

You may need some practice and even some guidance in adapting the self-testing habit to fit your style, but research shows that your efforts will pay off in your quest to become a successful student. Box 17 summarizes how to apply the self-testing habit.

Box 17 Applying the Self-Testing Habit	
Do this:	**Not this:**
Spend some of your study time answering questions on the material you studied.	Spend all your study time reviewing the material or even reviewing correct answers to questions.

Sources

Brown, P. C., Roediger, H. L., & McDaniel, M. A. (2014). *Make it stick: The science of successful learning.* Cambridge, MA: Harvard University Press.

Dunlosky, J., Rawson, K. A., Marsh, E. J., Nathan, M. J., & Willingham, D. T. (2013). Improving students' learning with effective learning techniques: Promising directions from cognitive and educational psychology. *Psychological Science in the Public Interest, 14*(1), 4–58.

Fiorella, L., & Mayer, R. E. (2015). *Learning as a generative activity: Eight learning strategies that promote understanding.* New York: Cambridge University Press.

Successful Habit #18

Explain the Material to Yourself

Learning with Laundry

It is laundry day for Larry. He carries his basketful of dirty clothes down to the laundry room in the basement of his apartment building, puts his clothes into the washer, adds some detergent, puts in a pocketful of coins, and presses the start button. Now, he will have a solid 20 minutes to study for his upcoming microbiology exam. No one else is there so he plops down on a nearby bench and opens his notes and his textbook and starts to read over the material, lecture by lecture. When the washer stops, he moves his clothes to the dryer and continues his reading for another 20 minutes. In this way, Larry sits quietly and reads every word of his notes. What a perfect way to use laundry time to study, Larry thinks to himself.

Across the quad, it is also laundry day for Linda. She also brings her dirty clothes down to the laundry room in the basement of her apartment building and gets them running through the washer and dryer. Like her classmate across the quad, she wants to use her laundry time to study for her upcoming microbiology exam. There is no one else down there so she places her notebook and textbook on top of a dryer, and using the top of the dryer as a sort of podium, she starts to give a lecture on the material, especially the important parts that need some clarification. Happily standing at her makeshift podium, she explains aloud the important material for each of the lectures that will be covered on the exam, by clarifying anything that is confusing and showing how the material fits together. For Linda, it is fun to take the role of the teacher in trying to explain the material, while her clothes go around in the machines.

What Do You Think?

Both Larry and Linda are to be congratulated for their dedication in using laundry time to study, but who is making the best use of their study time? Place a check mark next to each statement you agree with:

☐ A. Larry, because he is studying exactly what the instructor said and what was printed in the textbook.

☐ B. Not Linda, because she is spending her time making things up rather than focusing on the material.

☐ C. Linda, because by putting the material in her words she needs to decide what is important, explain how it fits together, and think more deeply about it.

☐ D. Not Larry, because he is likely to resort to memorizing isolated factoids.

If you checked A or B, you favored Larry's approach. Larry certainly looks like he is doing the right thing by focusing on the actual words of the instructor (at least as they are recorded in Larry's lecture notes) and the textbook author (at least based on Larry's skimming of each chapter). Reading over your notes and textbook chapters is certainly a worthwhile first step, but for studying that will lead to deep understanding, you might want to add a more active learning strategy.

If you checked C or D, you favored Linda's approach. Linda's approach may seem a little goofy, and might need some explaining if someone walked into the laundry room, but it represents an approach that can keep Linda more cognitively active, allowing her to learn more deeply.

What Linda is doing is called *self-explaining*. In self-explaining, you try to explain material to yourself usually through talking. Your monologue can include explaining how important systems work, raising questions, and reconciling any discrepancies that you find in the text or between the text and your prior knowledge. Research shows that self-explaining often is an effective learning strategy (Dunlosky, Rawson, Marsh, Nathan, & Willingham, 2013; Fiorella & Mayer, 2015; Rittle-Johnson & Loehr, 2017).

How does self-explaining work? Self-explaining is effective when it primes your appropriate cognitive processing, such as paying attention to the relevant material, mentally organizing it into a coherent structure, and integrating it with related prior knowledge activated from your long-term memory (Fiorella & Mayer, 2015). First, as you choose what to explain you are selecting the relevant material in the lesson. Second, when you explain to yourself, you need to put different pieces of information together, including reconciling two seemingly contradictory pieces of information. Third, when you explain to yourself, you need to put things in your words, which encourages you to relate the material to your relevant prior knowledge. In summary, you cause yourself to process the material more deeply when you self-explain, such as giving yourself a mini-lecture on the material.

Self-explaining Habit

The tale of Larry and Linda is not just about airing dirty laundry, but rather suggests another learning strategy for your successful student toolbox—*self-explaining*. Self-explaining involves explaining to yourself some of the important parts of the material you are studying. For your consideration, I offer the *self-explaining habit: People learn better when they explain main parts of the lesson content to themselves by elaborating on the material in their own words.* If you want to be a successful student—one who tries to make sense of the material—then self-explaining belongs in your toolbox of study strategies.

Don't get me wrong, there is nothing wrong with reading over your notes as a first step in studying. However, you are on the road to becoming an unsuccessful student if you do not follow-up with a more active learning strategy such as explaining confusing parts of the material to yourself. You might think that reading every word in your notes makes you a fine student, especially when you do it in your spare time, but actually you are acting like an unsuccessful student if that is all you do. You are acting like a successful student if you try to identify important material that you need to understand better, confusing or conflicting parts that need to reconciled, isolated parts that need to be connected, and interesting parts that need to be related to what you already know. Once you find parts of your notes that are worthy of further sense-making on your part, you can engage in the enjoyable task of self-explaining. This is the approach of a successful student.

I must admit that I particularly like the lecture-with-laundry version of self-explaining because this is how I spent many fine hours during my own college years. However, you may want to adapt the self-explaining strategy to a setting and style that makes you comfortable, such as talking about the material as you sit in a comfortable chair at home or under a tree in the woods or even by making short videos of your mini-lectures using the camera on your cell phone, tablet, laptop, or desktop computer. No matter how you self-explain, the goal is still the same: to help you work harder to make sense of the material so you are sure you understand it. Sometimes you just don't know how well you know material until you try to explain it to yourself.

Learning by self-explaining is closely related to a technique called *elaborative interrogation*. In elaborative interrogation, you ask yourself a predetermined question (such as some form of a "why" question) for sentences in a list or passage. For example, if the sentence says, "The hungry man got into the car," you could try to answer the question, "Why did he get into the car?" I do not emphasize elaborative interrogation in this chapter because it has been shown to be effective mainly for remembering isolated facts and for younger students (Dunlosky, Rawson, Marsh, Nathan, & Willingham, 2013), but you may be able to adapt elaborative interrogation for your own purposes.

So What Should I Do?

To get the most out of the self-explaining habit, I offer the following recommendations:

1. Allocate a portion (even a small portion) of your study time to self-explaining, to be used as you review your notes or textbook. Generally, you can do your self-explaining orally.
2. Find your favorite spot for self-explaining, such as in an empty laundry room, on a secluded bench in the woods, or in a comfy chair in your room. Spread out your notes from a textbook chapter or lecture, and mark the important, complicated, or confusing parts that need explaining. Then, go ahead and explain those parts to yourself, perhaps as a mini-lecture. If you prefer you can stand up as you talk. Alternatively, you could record your mini-lecture using your computer's web-cam or your cell phone's camera.

3. Look over your notes and mark spots to elaborate with prompts involving "why?" or "how?" or "what are the implications?" Then, go ahead and give a brief oral explanation for each elaborative prompt, using the procedure in the previous recommendation.

4. Use self-explaining in conjunction with other learning habits such as highlighting (i.e., Successful Habit #12) or outlining (i.e., Successful Habit #15) by basing your self-explanations on notes or a textbook chapter that you have already highlighted or outlined.

The self-explaining habit may seem unfamiliar at first, but with some practice and even some guidance, you will get better at it. Research shows that your efforts will be worth it. Box 18 summarizes the do's and don'ts of self-explaining.

Box 18 How to Apply the Self-Explaining Habit	
Do This:	**Not this:**
Explain the material you studied to yourself by elaborating in your own words.	Review the material without explaining it or elaborating on it.

Sources

Dunlosky, J., Rawson, K. A., Marsh, E. J., Nathan, M. J., & Willingham, D. T. (2013). Improving students' learning with effective learning techniques: Promising directions from cognitive and educational psychology. *Psychological Science in the Public Interest, 14*(1), 4–58.

Fiorella, L., & Mayer, R. E. (2015). *Learning as a generative activity: Eight learning strategies that promote understanding.* New York: Cambridge University Press.

Rittle Johnson, B., & Loehr, A. M. (2017). Instruction based on self-explanation. In R. E. Mayer & P. A. Alexander (Eds.), *Handbook of research on learning and instruction* (2nd ed; pp. 349–364). New York: Routledge.

Successful Habit #19

Try Explaining Material to Others

Meet Me at Moe's

Patty and Paul have decided to form a two-person study group for a workshop they are taking on "Learning to Learn." The workshop involves reading the book you are holding, but in spite of the excellent writing, Patty recognizes that there are a few points that are not clear to her and Paul also has his own problems with a few other points.

They have decided to meet on Tuesday afternoon at 4:00 in Moe's Coffee Shop to go over the material. They each have agreed to bring three things they do not understand so well, including showing where it is discussed in the book. Their plan is to take turns in the role of student and teacher, with one of them describing a point that needs to be clarified (as a student) and the other one trying to explain it (as a teacher).

Patty starts with saying, "I am not sure what stereotype threat is." She shows Paul the paragraph in the book where the term is discussed. Paul reads the material aloud with her, trying to elaborate on it and give some concrete examples. Paul is enthused by his ability to explain the term and Patty is relieved to see she actually understood it better than she thought.

Next it is Paul's turn. He turns to the section on mapping that mentions a "matrix" and says: "I do not understand how mapping would work for a matrix. The book only gives an example of a hierarchy." Patty reads the sentences about mapping with a matrix and tries to elaborate as she reads. She then makes up an example text that involves comparing two items and draws a matrix to show how you could map it. "Thanks," says Paul, "now I get it." Patty smiles at the success of her explanation.

Patty and Paul continue until they have exhausted their lists of points that need clarifying, and they have had their fill of Moe's excellent coffee. On their way out Patty and Paul notice that their friends and fellow workshop attendees, Quincy and Quenta, are in another corner of Moe's Coffee Shop, each reviewing the book on their own. Patty and Paul are excited to tell their friends about their study group, but Quincy and Quenta say they do not think a study group is a good idea. "You waste your time listening to someone else's problems or talking about something you already know," Quincy says. "Yeah, I'd much rather spend my time reviewing the book on my own so I can focus on what I need to study," Quenta adds.

Watch Your Ps and Qs

Who is right? Is it better to study on your own or with someone else? Please put a check next to the statements you agree with:

☐ A. I would rather study by myself so I can focus on what I want to study.

☐ B. When you are in a study group, you spend a lot of time dealing with questions that you can already answer, so you don't learn anything new.

☐ C. The act of explaining something to someone else helps me understand it better.

☐ D. The requirement to pinpoint issues that need to be clarified helps me assess my own learning.

Some students like to study alone. If you are one of them, you probably checked options A and B. There is certainly nothing wrong with studying alone, as expressed in option A, especially if you employ some of the habits described in other chapters in this book. I also can understand why you picked option B, if you have experienced ineffective peer tutoring situations in the past. For example, some instructors are fond of stopping their lecture and asking you to turn to the person next to you and discuss the material for a few minutes. Sometimes that discussion is awkward, vacuous, or not at all focused on the material. Similarly, working in groups in a classroom can be done poorly so that you really do not get anything out of it. If you chose option B because you have had sub-optimal experiences in group study, I certainly understand. There is substantial research evidence that not all group study experiences are effective (Fiorella & Mayer, 2014; Slavin, 2017).

However, let me ask you to consider the potential reflected in options C and D. In support of option C, there is substantial research evidence that you can develop a better understanding of the material when you explain it to someone else, which can be called *learning by teaching* (Fiorella & Mayer, 2013, 2014, 2015). Concerning option D, there is also some evidence that you learn better when you are asked to find parts of the lesson that are not clear to you (Fiorella & Mayer, 2015). This is the first step in what I call *self-explaining* in the previous chapter. Identifying parts of a lesson that you do not fully understand has been shown to be an important metacognitive skill called *comprehension monitoring*. When you have to select portions of a lesson that you need help with, you are engaging in comprehension monitoring—and thereby increasing your skill at monitoring and controlling your learning processes.

Overall, if you prefer the Qs (Quincy and Quenta) to the Ps (Patsy and Paul) you run the risk of becoming an unsuccessful student. You may prefer other strategies because you simply do not want to go out of your way to engage in group study. That is fine, but to develop your skill at becoming a successful student, you also may want to accept the opportunity to explain the material to others when that opportunity presents itself to you.

Learning by Teaching

Learning by teaching occurs when you teach others about material that you have studied previously. How does the learning strategy of learning by teaching work? First, it helps you identify the most important elements to put in your explanation—corresponding to the cognitive process of selecting. Second, it encourages you to put the elements together into a coherent structure that makes sense to someone—corresponding to the cognitive process of organizing. Third, it causes you to use your relevant prior knowledge to put the explanation in your own words—corresponding to the cognitive process of integrating. In short, when you explain material that you have studied to someone else, you must engage in the cognitive processes that lead to deep learning—selecting the relevant material in the lesson, mentally organizing it into a coherent structure, and integrating it with your relevant prior knowledge. For this reason, I offer the *learning-by-teaching habit* (or simply the *teaching habit*): *People learn better when they explain material they have studied to others.*

Learning by teaching is a key component in instructional practices that go under the names of *peer tutoring, cooperative learning*, and *collaborative learning*. In each of these approaches, you study in a group of your peers and have opportunities to explain material to them. There are possible pitfalls when group learning situations are not properly structured and guided, when you do not have appropriate training and practice in group learning, when you focus on reciting individual facts rather than making sense of the material, and when you simply are not motivated to engage in group learning. In short, to become a successful student, you have to learn how to use the learning by teaching strategy effectively, and particularly, to stay focused on the task of improving your understanding of the material.

So What Should I Do?

Here are a few recommendations for how to get the most out of the teaching habit:

1. You will need to allocate some time and commit yourself wholeheartedly to group study. This includes agreeing to the norms of participation for your study group, such as taking turns asking and answering questions, building on each other's explanations without being negative, maintaining a respectful atmosphere, and staying focused on the task. Have a system that includes everyone, such as taking turns. Create a manageable group, such as a group of two, three, four, five, or six people.

2. Begin by selecting target material such as a chapter in the textbook or a lecture. Take a moment to review your notes, and mark any parts that you think need further explanation or elaboration or clarification. Each person takes a turn explaining one part of the material, and each other member of the group can add further elaboration.

3. Begin by selecting target material such as a chapter in a textbook or a lecture. Take a moment to review

your notes and jot down a few questions that you need some help with. Each person takes a turn asking a question, and someone else answers the question. Other group members elaborate on the answer.

4. Begin with a set of challenging questions based on the target material. For each question, each team member takes a turn at contributing to an answer, perhaps building on the previous member's answer. A group scribe tries to create summaries of each contribution on a board, poster paper, or computer screen. The group then works on combining the contributions into a coherent written answer. On each subsequent question, the order of contributions is changed based on a system that insures everyone gets a chance at going first.

If you are a little shy or just prefer to study alone, then learning by teaching may take some getting used to. I must admit that I prefer to study alone, but I also know there is much to be gained by discussing the material with others. The material can become clearer and better clarified when you have to explain it or compare your explanation to other people's explanations. Box 19 summarizes the do's and don'ts of applying the teaching habit.

BOX 19 How to Apply the Teaching Habit	
Do this:	**Not this:**
When you are in a study group, be sure to explain confusing material to others.	When you are in a study group, sit quietly and get answers for your questions.

Sources

Fiorella, L., & Mayer, R. E. (2013). The relative benefits of learning by teaching and teaching expectancy. *Contemporary Educational Psychology, 38,* 281–288.

Fiorella, L., & Mayer, R. E. (2014). The role of explanations and expectations in learning by teaching. *Contemporary Educational Psychology, 39,* 75–85.

Fiorella, L., & Mayer, R. E. (2015). *Learning as a generative activity: Eight learning strategies that promote understanding.* New York: Cambridge University Press.

Slavin, R. E. (2017). Instruction based on cooperative learning. In R. E. Mayer & P. A. Alexander (Eds.), *Handbook of research on learning and instruction* (2nd ed.; pp. 388–404). New York: Routledge.

Successful Habit #20

Engage in Hands-On Activities

The Perfect Classroom

Welcome to Mr. C's chemistry class. Even though this is an early morning class, all the students are sitting still in their seats, facing the front of the room, without any wiggles or yawns. Today's lesson is on the structure of Mr. C's favorite molecules. Mr. C draws a diagram of a molecule on the board and explains it by showing the class a ball-and-stick model, which he manipulates and points to as he lectures away about the atoms and the connections between them. The students watch attentively with their eyes on the instructor. They all look like terrific learners to Mr. C. What could be a better way to learn from the demonstration than to sit still and watch carefully?

Next door is Ms. C's chemistry class. She starts out with the same molecule, and essentially goes through the same demonstration as Mr. C, except in addition she gives each student their own ball-and-stick model for each molecule. She asks the students to follow along as she constructs, manipulates, and points to parts of the model that correspond to parts of the drawn diagram on the board. These students are learning by enacting—that is, physically moving objects as they learn. Ms. C thinks her students will learn better by physically manipulating their molecule model along with her, even though it might require a bit more activity from them.

Which Classroom Learns Better?

As you look at the students in these two classes, which ones do you think are exhibiting the best learning strategies? Please place a check mark next to the statements you agree with concerning how to learn from a presentation:

☐ A. It is best to focus your attention on the instructor as he or she presents a demonstration, and not waste your time doing anything else.

☐ B. It can be helpful to "learn with your body" by physically manipulating objects that correspond to what the instructor is demonstrating.

You might look at Mr. C's class and think, "This is an excellent class. The students are exhibiting top-notch study skills by focusing their attention on the instructor." When you look at Ms. C's class you might think, "Those students are distracting themselves by fiddling around with the models. They are probably missing out on seeing what the instructor is doing." If so, you probably checked option A.

However, when I look at what the students are doing in Mr. C's class I am glad that the students are "on task" but still I am a bit concerned. Looking is not the same as learning. Simply sitting still and looking at the instructor is a learning strategy that can turn you into an unsuccessful student. In addition to watching the instructor, students need to engage in appropriate cognitive processing during learning. When I look at what the students are doing in Ms. C's class I am hopeful that they are learning more deeply. When they use the models to follow the demonstration, they must pay close attention and also translate what they see into actions—which causes them to learn more deeply. To avoid the trap of "watching without learning" you need to apply successful learning strategies that cause you to process more deeply. Learning by enacting is one such strategy. This is why I opt for option B.

Learning by Enacting

The *learning-by-enacting habit* (or simply the *enacting habit*) is: *People learn better when they engage in task-relevant movements during learning.* When you learn by enacting, you engage in movements during learning that help you make sense of the material. In the example of the chemistry class, the movements can involve manipulating a model of a molecule in sync with the instructor (Stull, Gainer, & Hegarty, 2018). In viewing a multimedia lesson on how a device works (such as a tire pump), the movements can involve manipulating a clear plastic model of the device (Mayer, Mathias, & Wetzell, 2002).

In learning computer programming from a manual, you might act out each command by physically writing or erasing a number from a portion of a whiteboard arranged to represent a memory space or moving a pointer down a to-do list (Mayer, 1975). In learning a mathematical procedure such as how to carry out addition and subtraction of signed numbers, this might involve moving a bunny along a number line within an online tutoring system (Moreno & Mayer, 1999).

I suggest that you add the learning-by-enacting habit to your toolbox of learning strategies. Learning by enacting has been shown to be an effective learning strategy (Fiorella & Mayer, 2015; Lillard, 2016; Mayer, 1975; Mayer, Mathias, & Wetzell, 2002; Moreno & Mayer, 1999; Stull, Gainer, & Hegarty, 2018). It can be especially effective for students who possess a high level of prior knowledge or who have sufficient practice and guidance in how their movements are related to the underlying concepts (Fiorella & Mayer, 2015; Moreno & Mayer, 1999). However, I also suggest caution in applying the learning-by-enacting habit because you do not want the movements to add extra commotion that distracts you from the key content in the lesson. Hands-on activity does not guarantee that you will engage in appropriate cognitive activity, so you need to make sure your behavioral activity translates into deep cognitive activity. If learning by enacting causes you to lose track of the lesson, you might want to switch to a more manageable learning strategy. However, in some situations sitting still as you watch is not the best way to learn.

So What Should I Do?

The enacting habit may seem a little unusual for you, and moving around as you study may be outside your comfort zone. However, for certain kinds of material, you might want to try a small dose of learning by enacting. If you decide to give this a try, here are my suggestions for how to be most effective:

1. Look over your notes or textbook pages for the material you want to study and mark any parts that could be acted out. Maybe start with just one part. Gather or create any concrete objects you will need. Then, as you read over the material aloud or explain the material aloud, move the objects (or your body) in sync with each step you describe. For example, to explain how to solve $3 - -2 =$ ___, you can create a number line board with successive squares ranging from −10 to +10. Find a small token—such as a small plastic bunny—that can fit in one of the squares. Say "3" and put the bunny (facing toward you) in the +3 square. Then say "minus" and turn the bunny to face toward the negative side of the number line (i.e., to the left). Then say "negative 2" and jump the bunny backward two steps so it lands on the +5 square. Finally, say "the answer is 5."

2. As you watch a video showing how to do something, have the same kind of concrete materials with you and carry out the steps in sync with the video. For example, in a video that shows how to thread a

sewing machine, actually have a sewing machine in front of you so you can physically carry out each step described in the video.

3. As you watch an instructor give a demonstration, carry out the same demonstration with corresponding materials at your desk. For example, in a chemistry class, an instructor may use a ball-and-stick model to explain what happens when two molecules combine, and you can carry out the same steps with ball-and-stick materials at your desk.

You may be able to devise ways to use the enacting habit that fit with the material you are studying and with your personal preferences for how to study. The enacting habit may apply to only a limited amount of your material so you will need to be careful to pinpoint where it best applies—such as for acting out a process. Box 20 summarizes the do's and don'ts of applying the enacting habit.

Box 20 How to Apply the Enacting Habit	
Do this:	**Not this:**
Act out the material using concrete objects or body movements.	Always sit still as you study.

Sources

Fiorella, L., & Mayer, R. E. (2015). *Learning as a generative activity: Eight learning strategies that promote understanding.* New York: Cambridge University Press.

Lillard, A. S. (2016). *Montessori: The science behind the genius*. New York: Oxford University Press.

Mayer, R. E. (1975). Different problem-solving competencies established in learning computer programming with and without meaningful models. *Journal of Educational Psychology, 67*, 725–734.

Mayer, R. E., Mathias, A., & Wetzell, K. (2002). Fostering understanding of multimedia messages through pretraining: Evidence for a two-stage theory of mental model construction. *Journal of Experimental Psychology: Applied, 8*, 147–154.

Moreno, R. & Mayer, R. E. (1999). Multimedia-supported metaphors for meaning making in mathematics. *Cognition and Instruction, 17*, 215–248.

Stull, A. T., Gainer, M. J., & Hegarty, M. (2018). Learning by enacting: The role of embodiment in chemistry education. *Learning and Instruction, 55*, 80–92.

Conclusion

20 Habits for Successful Studying

Three Steps in Learning to Learn

In this book I have suggested three steps in your quest to become a successful student. These steps involve forming motivational habits, management habits, and learning habits.

Your first step in becoming a successful student is to develop strategies that stimulate your will to learn. These are intended to help you build the motivation you need to take on challenging learning situations and persist with them. I call them *motivational habits*—or motivational strategies—because they are aimed at giving you the will to exert the effort needed to understand the material. This corresponds to the MOTIVE component of MOM described in the introduction.

Your second step in becoming a successful student is to create a climate that gives you the best possible opportunity to learn. I call these *management habits*—or management strategies—because they help you manage your time, your external environment, and your attention so you are ready to focus on the learning task. This corresponds to the OPPORTUNITY component of MOM described in the introduction.

Finally, your third step in becoming a successful student is to equip yourself with a set of powerful techniques to support your learning that you can use to make sense of the material you study. I call these *learning habits*—or learning strategies—because they help you engage in cognitive processes during learning that result in deep learning outcomes. In particular, you will need learning strategies that allow you to engage in *generative learning*—in which you carry out appropriate cognitive processing such as attending to relevant material in the lesson (i.e., *selecting*), mentally organizing it into a coherent structure that makes sense to you (i.e., *organizing*), and integrating it with your relevant prior knowledge activated from long-term memory (i.e., *integrating*). This corresponds to the MEANS component of MOM described in the introduction.

Four Motivational Habits that Foster Your Effort to Learn

Tables 1 and 2 list four motivational habits that are intended to prepare your will to learn, so you have the motivation to take on and stick with the task of learning something new. If just getting started to study is a daunting task for you, then you need to equip yourself with some effective motivational habits. If you feel like giving up on studying before you have learned the material, then you need to equip yourself with some effective motivational habits. Activating your motivation to learn is the first step in becoming a successful learner. You need the motivation to exert effort to learn even when the material is hard to understand. This includes exerting effort to figure out which learning strategies will be helpful to you on the task at hand.

Without the will to exert effort to learn you could easily fall into the trap of being an unsuccessful student. Where does the will to exert effort come from? As described in Part 1 of this book on MOTIVE TO LEARN, four sources of your motivation to exert effort are your interests, your goals, your beliefs, and your response to threats.

As shown in the first lines of Tables 1 and 2, motivation to learn comes from your own personal interest and curiosity. In short, your motto should be: "I am curious about this." Before you begin studying, take a few moments to explain to yourself why this material could be valuable to you and what you find interesting about it. If you find the material uninteresting and useless, you are less likely to work hard to understand it and less likely to be a successful student.

As shown in the second lines of Tables 1 and 2, your will to exert effort also comes from your personal goal for learning. If your personal goal is to master the material, your motto might be something like: "I want to understand this." This can be called a *mastery goal* and it is the kind of goal you should have for successful studying. If your goal is to excel above others by getting a high grade, you have a type of *performance goal*. This also can be motivating, but it is most long-lasting if combined with a mastery goal. If your personal goal mainly is to avoid doing poorly, you are more likely to stop working hard, and thus become an unsuccessful student.

As shown in the third lines of Tables 1 and 2, another way to motivate yourself to work hard is to develop productive beliefs about yourself as a learner. You need chances to see that if you work hard enough, you actually can master the material. Try to see yourself as a competent learner who is capable of learning the material you are studying. If you think learning is determined by

Table 1 Four Motivational Habits of Successful Students

Name	Description	Motto
Value habit	You learn better when you value and are personally interested in the material.	I am curious about this.
Goal habit	You learn better when your goal is to master the material you are studying.	I want to understand this.
Belief habit	You learn better when you believe that you can learn if you exert effort, that failures and successes depend mainly on your effort rather than fixed ability, and that you can improve your mind through working hard.	I can do this if I try.
Threat habit	You learn better when you avoid feeling threatened by other people's opinions of your ability to learn.	No one can make me give up.

effort, you are more likely to work harder when things get tough. These are the beliefs of a successful student. Your motto should be: "I can do this if I try." If you think learning is determined mainly by your ability, you are less likely to exert effort when things get tough and more likely to fall into the abyss of being an unsuccessful student.

Finally, as shown in the fourth lines of Tables 1 and 2, another important aspect of motivation involves how

Table 2 Examples of Four Motivational Habits of Successful Students

Name	General example	Specific example
Value habit	Take a moment to determine how the material you are studying might have some value for you.	For a lesson on the human digestive system, see that it could help you with your quest to eat nutritious foods.
Goal habit	Spell out your mastery goals for the class and how you assess your progress.	Write down your learning objectives for a lesson.
Belief habit	Strengthen your belief in yourself as a competent learner who can succeed if you try hard enough.	Write a brief note to yourself about your ability to learn the material by using effective study strategies.
Threat habit	Do not buy into stereotypes that other people may have about your ability to learn the material.	When you find anything that is hard for you, plan out the learning strategies you can apply.

you respond to the demotivating opinions of others. *Stereotype threat* occurs when you see yourself as a member of a group that other people think will perform poorly. When a young woman's friend says, "Why would you want to go into physics? That's no place for you," she can respond by working hard and never losing confidence in herself. Your motto as a successful student should be: "No one can make me give up." Once you let other people define who you are as a learner, you may find yourself slipping down the slope to becoming an unsuccessful student.

Six Management Habits that Create a Climate for Learning

Tables 3 and 4 list six management habits intended to prepare a climate in which you can flourish as a student. Becoming a successful student requires that you hone your management skills—including how you manage your time, manage your external environment, and manage your internal environment. In preparing your learning environment, you will need the time to learn, a place to learn, and a mind ready to learn. The six management habits described in Part 2 of this book, under the heading of OPPORTUNITY TO LEARN, are intended to equip you with the strategies you will need to prepare a climate for successful learning. The time, spacing, and interleaving habits help you manage your time; the multitasking habit helps you manage your physical environment; and the anxiety and mindfulness habits help you manage your internal environment (i.e., your attention).

If you try to study in a climate that is not conducive to learning—such as cramming at the last minute, texting your friends as you study, or studying with a panicked mind full of worry—you will be displaying the characteristics of an unsuccessful student. How do you create a climate for successful learning? The first three rows in Tables 3 and 4 summarize three habits for managing your time, the fourth row in Tables 3 and 4 summarizes a habit for managing your external environment, and the last two rows in Tables 3 and 4 summarize two habits for managing your internal environment.

Let's start with the time habit in the first rows of Tables 3 and 4. An important step in becoming a successful student is to set aside dedicated time for studying. To master this habit, your personal motto should be something like: "I make time to study." Specific study periods should be part of your weekly schedule. If your approach to studying does not include a schedule for when you will be studying, then your approach corresponds to that of an unsuccessful student. Successful students understand that what you learn is directly related to the amount of time in which you engage in productive studying.

Just allocating time for studying is a good first step, but you also need to develop habits for how to use that time effectively. As summarized in the second rows of Tables 3 and 4, when you apply the spacing habit, you study material in many sessions over time rather than all at once just before the exam. Your motto as a successful student is something like: "I don't wait until the last minute." If you prefer to cram at the last minute, you are displaying the habit of an unsuccessful student. You can avoid this situation by scheduling multiple study periods that are distributed across the week or term, and thus display the habits of a successful student.

Similarly, as shown in the third rows of Tables 3 and 4 on the interleaving habit, an effective way for you to manage your time is to alternate among several different topics within each study session, especially if the time period is long. Your motto as a successful student could be: "I take turns studying different topics." If you spend hours studying the same material, your studying can become less effective. When you break it up with studying different types of material, perhaps from different courses, your studying can become more effective.

Once you have scheduled your time appropriately, you need to find a place to study—somewhere free of distractions. This is accomplished with the multitasking habit, as described in the fourth rows of Tables 3 and 4. Your motto as a successful student could be: "I create a distraction-free zone." If you love to study with loud music playing or the big game blaring on a large-screen TV, or you love to study with your cell phone or laptop open to allow you to participate in the latest tweets or text messaging conversations, then you are not doing a good job of creating a distraction-free zone. To avoid these distractions and develop your habit of not multitasking, you can add a personal motto: "I don't multitask." Your best bet is to create or find a space—either at home or somewhere on or near campus—where you know you can always go to study in peace.

Once you have the time and place to study, you also need to make sure you have a mind that is ready to study. As summarized in the fifth rows of Tables 3 and 4, the anxiety habit involves freeing your mind of negative thoughts and worries so you can focus your attention on the task of studying the material. Your personal motto here is: "I free my mind of worry." Admittedly, managing your anxiety can be a difficult task that requires more than telling

Table 3 Six Management Habits of Successful Students

Name	Description	Motto
Time habit	You learn better when you spend time engaged in focused study.	I make time to study.
Space habit	You learn better when you spread out study sessions over time (rather than concentrating all your studying in one long session).	I don't wait until the last minute.
Interleaving habit	You learn better when you alternate studying among difference topics in a session (rather than just studying one topic).	I take turns studying different topics.
Multitasking habit	You learn better when you avoid external distractions during studying.	I create a distraction-free zone. I don't multitask.
Anxiety habit	You learn better when your mind is not clouded with negative thoughts of worry.	I free my mind of worry.
Mindfulness habit	You learn better when you focus your attention on the task of studying.	I focus my attention.

Table 4 Examples of Six Management Habits of Successful Students

Name	General example	Specific example
Time habit	Plan your schedule to include study time.	On your calendar, post sessions to study specific material.
Space habit	Plan your schedule to space out studying across multiple sessions.	On your calendar, post many sessions for studying across the entire term.
Interleaving habit	Plan your schedule to include multiple topics in each session.	On your calendar, for each session indicate specific material from multiple topics.
Multitasking habit	Find or create a place to study that is free of distractions, loud music, interruptions, and intrusions from personal devices.	Turn off your cell phone when you are studying and keep it off.
Anxiety habit	Clear your mind of negative thoughts of worry.	Write a paragraph that summarizes your feelings. Give yourself a brief pep talk.
Mindfulness habit	Keep your attention on the learning task.	Clear your mind through meditation.

yourself, "Don't worry about it." However, if you allow your negative thoughts to dominate your study period, you will diminish your chances of successful studying. Just putting in time is not good enough; to be a successful student you need to put in productive time—time when you are actively concentrating on the to-be-learned material.

Similarly, as summarized in the sixth rows of Tables 3 and 4, the mindfulness habit involves focusing your attention on the task of studying rather than letting your mind wander to other thoughts. Here your motto as a successful student is: "I focus my attention." Your attention is a precious resource that is crucial for successful studying. If you are thinking of why your friend snubbed you today or when you are going to run an errand, you are not thinking about the to-be-learned material. Learning to manage your attention during learning is a major challenge that can take years of training and practice, but this is a management habit that is central to your success as a student.

Ten Learning Habits that Foster Generative Learning

Now that you have created the motive and opportunity to learn, your next step is to apply some effective strategies for facilitating your learning. Tables 5 and 6 list ten learning habits of successful students that are intended to foster generative learning—that is, deep learning that leads to understanding. In generative learning you pay attention to the relevant material in the lesson (i.e., engage in the cognitive process of selecting), mentally organize it into a coherent structure that makes sense to you (i.e., engage in the cognitive process of organizing), and integrate the incoming information with relevant prior knowledge activated from long-term memory (i.e., engage in the cognitive process of integrating). Each of the ten learning habits (or learning strategies) is intended to prime these three cognitive processes as you study.

The ten learning habits—rereading, highlighting, pre-training, summarizing, mapping, drawing, self-testing, self-explaining, teaching, and enacting—correspond to Part 3 of this book on MEANS TO LEARN. If you do not use effective learning habits, you run the risk of learning in a rote way in which you try to remember the material as it was presented in the book or spoken in the lecture. This is an unsuccessful way to learn. If you equip yourself with a healthy collection from these ten learning habits, you will have the tools to successfully learn the material more deeply when you study—that is, to engage in generative learning. A successful way to learn is for you to apply one or more of these learning habits to fit your learning task.

The first three study habits for successful learning listed in Tables 5 and 6 are commonly used and you already may be using some of them: Rereading, highlighting, and pre-training (e.g., with flashcards). However, you can boost the usefulness of these study habits if you use them in conjunction with some of the more powerful techniques listed in the rest of the table. Let me show what I mean as we look at each of the "common three" study habits.

As shown in the first rows in Tables 5 and 6, rereading is a commonly used learning habit in which you read text more than once. To employ rereading to promote generative learning, you should try to detect parts of your textbook chapter or lecture notes that do not make sense to you or that need some clarification, and then be sure to reread those parts. Your motto as a successful student is: "I reread text that is confusing." To maximize its effectiveness, you can also use this habit in conjunction with others such as self-explaining or summarizing (described later in Tables 5 and 6). However, to be most effective, you probably do not want to blindly reread everything with equal emphasis, as that reflects the habit of an unsuccessful student.

As shown in the second rows of Tables 5 and 6, highlighting is another commonly used learning habit in which you underline or otherwise mark part of a text as you read. To use highlighting to promote generative learning, you should try to detect parts of your textbook chapter or lecture notes that are most important. Your motto as a successful student is: "I highlight important ideas." In order to increase the effectiveness of highlighting, you should use it in conjunction with other study habits such as to help you write a summary of the material (i.e., summarizing habit), to help you create an outline or mini-outlines of the material (i.e., mapping habit), or to form the basis of testing yourself (i.e., self-testing habit) or explaining the material to yourself (i.e., self-explaining habit). To be most effective, you probably want to use highlighting sparingly. Highlighting is intended to help you select and organize material so you can figure out what is important. If your whole book is highlighted you are not getting much benefit from highlighting, and you are on the road to becoming an unsuccessful student.

Another commonly used study habit is to use flashcards, which comes under the heading of pretraining in the third rows of Tables 5 and 6. In pretraining, you aim to memorize the key terms and their definitions or characteristics. Your motto as a successful student is: "I master key terms." For example, you could create flashcards with the term on one side and the definition on the other. Knowing the key terms can help you better understand the explanations in your book or notes because you do not have to use your limited processing capacity on trying to figure out what the terms mean. Memorizing definitions is just the first step in successful studying, because you also want to make sure you deeply understand the material through using some of the next study habits listed in Tables 5 and 6. If all you do is memorize, you are acting like an unsuccessful student.

The next three study habits for successful learning in Tables 5 and 6 involve translating from words (in your book or notes) to some other form of representation such as writing a concise summary (i.e., summarizing habit), creating an outline or knowledge map (i.e., mapping habit), or making an illustration (i.e., drawing habit). The first two habits include commonly used strategies—notetaking and outlining. You may be using these in some form already, but as you can see in this book, there are ways to use them most effectively.

Summarizing is one of the most powerful and easy-to-use study habits you can add to your collection as a successful student. As shown in the fourth rows of Tables 5 and 6, summarizing involves putting the main ideas of the lesson in your own words, by creating either a concise written summary or simply a concise oral summary.

Your motto should be: "I summarize in my own words." Summarizing works when it encourages you to attend to the important material (i.e., the cognitive process of selecting), organize it into a coherent structure that makes sense to you (i.e., the cognitive process of organizing), and relate it to your prior knowledge by putting it in your own words (i.e., the cognitive process of integrating). Summarizing does not mean just repeating or copying material word-for-word, and this would cause you to lose much of the effectiveness of summarizing. You might think of summarizing as notetaking, but it is a special kind of notetaking in which you focus on the main points and organize them into a coherent summary in your own words.

Mapping can also be a power tool for you in your quest to become a successful student. As shown in the fifth lines of Tables 5 and 6, mapping involves putting the main ideas in the lesson in a spatial arrangement such as an outline or knowledge map (e.g., a hierarchy, matrix, or flowchart). Your motto is: "I make outlines (or knowledge maps)." You may already engage in outlining, which is the most common form of mapping. Outlining can increase your understanding of the material when it is done well, and you can boost its effectiveness by using your outline in conjunction with other study habits such as summarizing or self-explaining. Learning to create knowledge maps may take a little more time, but can be a strong aid to you in mentally organizing the material, especially when used sparingly for key structures such as hierarchies, matrices, and flow charts. The goal is to help you select the important material and organize it and relate it to your prior knowledge. When you are not able to identify what is important, mapping is not going to be effective, so you may need some training and guidance to get started.

The next study habit—drawing—is less commonly used (and its cousin—imagining—is even less common), but it can be a big help to you especially for texts that describe all the parts in a system (such as the parts in the human circulatory system) or how a cause-and-effect system works (such as how the human circulatory system works). As described in the sixth rows of Tables 5 and 6, you create illustrations that depict the key material in a printed text, under the motto: "I make drawings." A close cousin of drawing is imagining, in which you simply create mental images (just like drawings) that depict the key material in a printed text, under the motto: "I make mental images." Drawing can help prime the cognitive processes selecting (i.e., you have to figure out what to put in your drawing), organizing (i.e., you have to arrange the parts spatially on the page), and integrating (i.e., you have to use your prior knowledge to translate from words to graphics). You will probably need some training and guidance to get the full benefit of drawing. Also, drawing can be cumbersome if you have to put too much mental effort into the mechanics of drawing, so you want to keep your drawings simple enough for you to make them easily.

The next four study habits for successful learning in Tables 5 and 6 involve elaborating on the material such as answering practice questions (i.e., self-testing habit), explaining the material to yourself (i.e., self-explaining habit), explaining it to someone else (i.e. teaching habit), or acting out the material with concrete objects (i.e., enacting habit).

Giving yourself a practice test on the material is a particularly effective study habit because you are practicing doing what you will have to do on the test—retrieving the relevant material from your memory and using it. As shown in the seventh rows of Tables 5 and 6, self-testing involves answering practice questions after you have studied the material. You may have already used some of the other study habits in Tables 5 and 6 such as rereading or highlighting or outlining, but with self-testing you are now practicing on answering questions like those that will be on the test. "I take practice tests," is your motto. If you can learn to test yourself on the material and you are willing to exert the effort to engage in the self-testing habit, you are well on your way to academic success. You probably will need some training and guidance in self-testing, but with practice and guidance you can hone this study habit to perfection. In my opinion, this is well worth your effort.

The self-explaining habit (often based on earlier highlighting or outlining) is my personal favorite for becoming a successful student. In self-explaining, as shown in the eighth rows of Tables 5 and 6, you look over your notes and/or book, and explain the material to yourself, usually aloud as if giving a mini-lecture to yourself.

"I explain to myself," is your motto. You need to be selective in what you are explaining, focusing on important systems or complex ideas and on points that were, at first, confusing to you. You will need to adapt self-explaining to your personal needs and style, but even if you use it only occasionally, it can improve your learning and become a welcome addition to your collection of study habits.

You may become involved in a study group in which you find yourself explaining some important material to another student. If so, you are not only helping your peer, you are also helping yourself understand the material better. According to the teaching habit, summarized in the ninth rows of Tables 5 and 6, you learn better when you explain material to others. When you engage in learning by teaching, your motto is: "I explain to others." Explaining to others causes you to figure out what you should say (i.e., selecting) and how to organize it (i.e., organizing) and even how to say it in a way others will understand (i.e., integrating). Some folks would rather study alone than with others, and sometimes study groups can degenerate into conversations that really are not relevant to learning the material. However, learning by teaching can be effective when collaborative studying is set up appropriately and everyone in the group has training and tries to make it work.

Finally, the tenth rows in Tables 5 and 6 describe the enacting habit, in which you engage in task-relevant movements to act out key material in the lesson.

Table 5 Ten Learning Habits of Successful Students

Name	Description	Motto
Rereading habit	You learn better when you reread parts of the text that need clarification or support other habits.	I reread text that is confusing.
Highlighting habit	You learn better when you correctly highlight important ideas in a printed text.	I highlight important ideas.
Pretraining habit	You learn better when you already know the key terms.	I master the key terms.
Summarizing habit	You learn better when you summarize the main ideas in a lesson in your own words.	I summarize in my own words.
Mapping habit	You learn better when you create an outline (or knowledge map) of the material in a lesson.	I make outlines (or knowledge maps).
Drawing habit	You learn better when you create drawings (or mental images) that depict the material in the text.	I make drawings (or mental images).
Self-testing habit	You learn better when you take practice tests on the material you studied.	I take practice tests.
Self-explaining habit	You learn better when you explain the core material to yourself by elaborating in your own words.	I explain to myself.
Teaching habit	You learn better when you explain the material you have studied to others.	I explain to others.
Enacting habit	You learn better when you engage in task-relevant movements during studying.	I act out the lesson.

Table 6 Examples of Ten Learning Habits of Successful Students

Name	General example	Specific example
Rereading habit	Stop when you realize you did not understand the sentence you just read and read it again (and if necessary reread related sentences) in order to make sure you understand.	You read a lesson on the brain that says, "After you practice a mental task, that results in a decrease in brain activity." At first you think it should increase activity so you reread the sentence and also find a related sentence that helps you see why less effort is required.
Highlighting habit	When you come to an important new term or piece of information, highlight it.	Use a yellow marker to highlight important steps in a process, and write in the step number in front of each.
Pretraining habit	Identify each key term and its definition and make sure you know them.	For a textbook chapter, create flash cards with the term on one side and the definition on the other.
Summarizing habit	Summarize the main ideas in a lesson in your own words.	Read over your class notes and create a written summary that contains the main points.
Mapping habit	Create an outline or knowledge map of the material in a lesson.	As you read over your textbook, create an outline, matrix, hierarchy, or flowchart in the margin that organizes the main elements.
Drawing habit	Create drawings (or mental images) that depict the material in the text.	As you read a lesson on how neurons communicate, draw a neuron and label the main parts.

Name	General example	Specific example
Self-testing habit	Take practice tests on the material you studied.	After you read a lesson on how neurons communicate, close the book, and write down all you can recall.
Self-explaining habit	Explain the material you studied to yourself by elaborating in your own words.	You take out your class notes on how neurons communicate, and give a mini-lecture to yourself.
Teaching habit	You explain the material you have studied to others.	In a study group, a peer says she didn't understand what the lecturer said about how neurons communicate, so you briefly explain it to her.
Enacting habit	Engage in task-relevant movements during studying.	You create hand gestures that correspond to each of the four steps of neural transmission that you just read about.

Sometimes enacting involves moving physical objects, under the motto: "I act out the lesson." The enacting habit may be new to you, unless perhaps you attended a Montessori school in which you worked with many concrete objects to represent mathematical concepts. For example, to understand how a computer program works you might act out each step in the program, such as writing a number in a simulated memory space or moving a pointer from the first command to the next one. At first, applying the enacting habit may seem awkward, but eventually I think you will see that it can be fun and help make abstract ideas more concrete for you.

Where Do I Go From Here?

If you have gotten this far in the book, I know you have what it takes to become a successful student. Even though this book is intended to improve your study habits, I want you to know that learning how to learn is something you can always get better at through your commitment to continuous self-improvement. Once you develop a study habit that works for you, you can refine it and adapt it to make it even more effective for you. You can be on the lookout for new study habits to add to your collection, perhaps by seeing what works for others or through continuing to read about study skills. I list some suggested readings at the end of this chapter.

Studying for academic success—the focus of this book—is only a start. I want you to become a lifelong learner, someone who is curious and interested in learning new things in school, at work, and in life. When you come upon a topic that you would like to learn about, you need the study habits that will help you accomplish this goal. The 20 study habits described in this book should serve you well, not only in school, but also in your everyday life or in your job. Improving your ability to learn is a lifelong commitment.

Becoming a better learner involves not only acquiring useful study habits, but learning when to use them and how to adjust them to the task at hand. When you monitor how your learning is going and adjust what you are doing accordingly, you are engaging in *metacognition*—thinking about your own cognitive processing. This puts you on the road to becoming a *self-regulated learner*—someone who takes responsibility for managing their own learning. Reading this book is a solid step in becoming a self-regulated learner.

As instruction migrates from print to online venues, your study habits should remain the same, but the way you implement them may change a little. Instead of reading a textbook, you might read an e-book on your laptop computer, tablet, or cell phone. Instead of sitting through a face-to-face lecture you might watch a video lecture at home on a personal device. Instead of writing out homework exercises, you might create and submit your work online. You might take an online course, learn from an online tutoring system, or play an interactive simulation game as a supplement to a traditional course you are taking. Developers are coming up with clever ways to implement learning strategies in these computer-based contexts. For example, you might be familiar with online systems for highlighting and notetaking for online lessons, or you might know some aps that allow you to annotate and index video lectures. In the coming years, research is needed to determine how best to use these kinds of online study aids, so you need to stay on the lookout.

If you make good use of this book, you can make yourself smarter. Intelligence is often defined as the ability to learn, and this book is intended to improve your effectiveness as a learner, so you can say this book is intended to help you get smarter. Your intelligence—including your ability to learn—has been shown to be one of your most important assets for success in school, at work, and in life. Along with *conscientiousness*—i.e., your commitment to working hard and persisting—your ability to learn and think (called *fluid intelligence*) and the knowledge you have acquired through learning (called *crystallized intelligence*) help you succeed on the tasks you want to accomplish (Martinez, 2000, 2013; Pellegrino & Hilton, 2012). If this book helps you become a better learner, I will consider it a success.

Sources

Martinez, M. E. (2000). *Education as the cultivation of human intelligence.* Mahwah, NJ: Erlbaum.

Martinez, M. E. (2013). *Future bright: A transforming vision of human intelligence.* New York: Oxford University Press.

Pellegrino, J. W., & Hilton, M. L. (2012). *Education for life and work: Developing transferrable knowledge and skills in the 21st century.* Washington, DC: National Academies Press.

Suggested Readings

In this section, I list some of my favorite publications on study skills.

Ambrose, S. A., Bridges, M. W., DiPiertro, M., Lovett, M. C., & Norman, M. K. (2010). *How learning works.* San Francisco: Jossey-Bass.

Boser, U. (2017). *Learn better.* New York: Rodale.

Bourne, L. E., & Healy, A. F. (2014). *Train your mind for peak performance.* Washington, DC: American Psychological Association.

Brown, P. C., Roediger, H. L., & McDaniel, M. A. (2014). *Make it stick: The science of successful learning.* Cambridge, MA: Harvard University Press.

Dunlosky, J., Rawson, K. A., Marsh, E. J., Nathan, M. J., & Willingham, D. T. (2013). Improving students' learning with effective learning techniques: Promising directions from cognitive and educational psychology. *Psychological Science in the Public Interest, 14*(1), 4–58.

Fiorella, L., & Mayer, R. E. (2015). *Learning as a generative activity: Eight learning strategies that promote understanding.* New York: Cambridge University Press.

Miyatsu, T., Nguyen, K., & McDaniel, M. A. (2018). Five popular study strategies: Their pitfalls and optimal implementations. *Perspectives on Psychological Science, 13,* 390–407.

Pashler, H., Bain, P. M., Bottge, B. A., Graesser, A., Koedinger, K., McDaniel, M., & Metcalfe, J. (2007). *Organizing instruction and study to improve student learning.* (IES Practice Guide, NCER 2007–2004). Washington, DC: National Center for Education Research.

Weinstein, C. E., & Mayer, R. E. (1985). The teaching of learning strategies. In M. C. Wittrock (ed.), *Handbook of Research on Teaching* (3rd ed; pp. 315–327). New York: Macmillan.

Index